Restoring Education
Central to American Greatness

Restoring Education: Central to American Greatness
Fifteen Principles That Liberated Mankind from the Politics of Tyranny

Copyright © 2011 David A. Norris

This book is a project of Heartland Foundation, Inc., 1616 Grand Avenue, Ames, Iowa 50010.
Chartered in Iowa February of 1981 as a 501 (c) (3) tax-deductible public service organization,
its purpose is an educational outreach that will advance traditional American values.

iUniverse books may be ordered through booksellers or by contacting:

iUniverse
1663 Liberty Drive
Bloomington, IN 47403
www.iuniverse.com
1-800-Authors (1-800-288-4677)

Because of the dynamic nature of the Internet, any Web addresses or links contained in this book
may have changed since publication and may no longer be valid. This being the case there will
be times when the reader will want to do an independent search to re-establish authenticity.

The views expressed in this work are solely those of the author and do not necessarily reflect
the views of the publisher, and the publisher hereby disclaims any responsibility for them.

Any people depicted in stock imagery provided by Thinkstock are models,
and such images are being used for illustrative purposes only.

Certain stock imagery © Thinkstock.

ISBN: 978-1-4502-8742-5 (pbk)
ISBN: 978-1-4502-8743-2 (cloth)
ISBN: 978-1-4502-8744-9 (ebk)

Library of Congress Control Number: 2011900969

Printed in the United States of America

iUniverse rev. date: 6/1/2011

Restoring Education
Central to American Greatness

Fifteen Principles That Liberated
Mankind from the Politics of Tyranny

DAVID A. NORRIS

iUniverse, Inc.
Bloomington

In this book, David Norris has again produced a significant piece of literature. With unimpeachable research, he documents the biblical principles for civil community upon which the nation was built, and then he exposes the betrayal of those sacred values by a small cadre of tenured radical educators.

Mr. Norris's background of experience has enabled him to identify the levers for restoring local citizen control. Restoring Education: Central to American Greatness *can be of great value to readers who are intent on restoring parental choice and reversing the harmful use of our schools by secular militants. I heartily recommend this book.*

—Ralph W. Hayes, who has done postgraduate studies
in the Humanities and holds a Doctorate in Education,
is a retired professor of education at Clearwater
Christian College, Clearwater, FL

A truly complete case for the godly biblical influences from which America's unique government and set of laws were patterned. David Norris brings the reader up to today's date on the history and status of the liberal educators and their philosophies so detrimental to our liberties. The deceptive retreat from reality and the invalid reasoning of postmodernists are exposed for what they are. Every God-honoring leader and Bible-believing church will benefit greatly by sharing the pro-American lexicon of this book. The well-cataloged references range from the Founding Fathers to today's best conservative jurists, whose writings are very useful for young people and adults alike.

—Lowell D. Bond, MD

David Norris has been given a wonderful gift of discernment and composition. His writings are so "on the money." He is right—we no longer have public education. In the behavioral and political sciences it has become government education comparable to the monopoly state doctrine that decimated Medieval Europe. Restoring Education: Central to American Greatness *is undoubtedly one of the best books ever written on the subject.*

—James C. Magee, PhD (biological science), and his wife, Lois, M.Ed., a public school teacher for thirty years

This book provides very valuable in-depth research showing that America's liberty and freedom stem from the application of unchanging biblical principles in the writing and application of the Declaration of Independence and the Constitution. The Norris book should be required reading in every college-level political science class.

—John Stormer, pastor, educator, author, served as chaplain for the Missouri state legislature for thirty-one years

I had met David Norris before he chaired the Jury's study of leftists working at Iowa State University. Reflective of campuses nationwide, their report has proven remarkably accurate. This book is a "must read" for anyone concerned about the deterioration of our higher education system. If we lose one more generation of students from lack of being taught the truths in our original documents, we will no longer be a Republic of free men.

—Charles D. Cowan, PhD, professor of electrical engineering at Iowa State University and Ohio Northern University

The Grand Jury Presentment is detailed in Appendix A:

"As one of the tens of thousands who admire the action of your Grand Jury, I wish to commend Foreman Norris and his jury for their courageous and true Americanism in focusing public attention on the perverted minority ... who would destroy what we have ... in America and deliver us unto our enemies." (E. Allen, Burlington, North Dakota, letter to the Nevada, Iowa *Journal*)

"OUT IN IOWA ... The jury's report said 'there is a need for increased emphasis at all levels of education of the American ideal. Our soldiers have been dying for this ideal. Education as never before should clearly teach it.' So say we." (from the *Boston Record*, printed in the *Ames Daily Tribune*)

Ames, Iowa–(AP)–The Grand Jury wants "moral pollution" ... "and defamation of our country" (in the Humanities curriculum) stopped. (*Denver Post*)

Convenient To Use

Indexed, Illustrated, Footnoted, Ideally Paragraphed ... **Outstanding Resource For**: Family Studies, Teachers, Students, Business, Political and Military Officials, School Boards, Public and Private Schools, Libraries ... **Beneficial In**: Letters to Editors, Presentations by Elected Officials, Judges, High School and College Reports, Government and Campaign Addresses, Sunday School God and Country Studies, Book Clubs ... **Scores of Quotations**: Founding Fathers, Founding Documents, Creation's God, the Bible, American Principles ...

With grateful thanks to the Founding Fathers
who, supported by their wives,
limited government for the sake of liberty.

This book is dedicated to
Americans—adults and youth,
native and foreign born

That we might train the young in our schools and
colleges, to understand and respect their heritage.

"Patriotism is as much a virtue as justice, and is as necessary for support of societies as the natural affection is for the support of families. The Amor Patriae is both moral and a religious duty. It comprehends not only the love of our neighbors but millions of our fellow creatures, not only the present but of future generations. This virtue we find constitutes a part of the first character of history."

—Dr. Benjamin Rush, essay on patriotism published in 1773. He was a delegate to the Continental Congress from Pennsylvania and signed the Declaration of Independence. A devout Christian, Rush established Dickinson College in Carlisle, Pennsylvania, and served as professor of medical theory and clinical practice at the University of Pennsylvania from 1791 to 1813.

Contents

Acknowledgments   xiii

Introduction: Reality   1

Part I: Government   **11**

Chapter 1   13
Immortal Principles Central to Liberty and American Greatness

Chapter 2   35
The Sovereignty of Man under the Impartial God of Creation over Government

Chapter 3   47
Man May Prosper in Freedom If He Chooses to Honor the Will of Creation's God

Chapter 4   58
America's Civic Religion and the Deeper Personal Faith of Our Nation's Founders

Chapter 5   69
Government by Written and Permanent Law

Chapter 6   73
Defilement of the Judiciary

Part II: Education   **91**

Chapter 7   93
Academic Freedom and Teacher Tenure History

Chapter 8   100
Consequences of the Unionization of Government Teachers

Chapter 9   105
The Education Nightmare

Chapter 10   110
Education That Is Profoundly American

Part III: Liberty and Responsibility   **115**

Chapter 11   117
Appeasement Will Not Work

Chapter 12   119
Our Strategy for Victory: Political Action—Citizen Power

Part IV: Supplemental Material   **129**

Appendix A   131
Grand Jury Presentment Problems in Higher Education

Appendix B   147
State of Iowa Bill of Rights

Appendix C   153
How Socialism Exploits Mankind

Appendix D   155
Citation Notes

Index   163

Acknowledgments

This book could not have been written without a record left by the Founding Fathers. Two documents, the Creator-based *Declaration of Independence* and the *Constitution,* are the cornerstones upon which government for the greatest nation on earth was developed. They reached beyond the failed practices of man to immortal values that make stability, liberty, and prosperity possible. In his July 4, 1821, oration as Secretary of State, John Quincy Adams (soon to become president) captured the foundation for American law: "It was the first solemn *Declaration* by a nation of the only *legitimate* foundation for civil government. It was the corner stone of the new fabric, destined to cover the surface of the globe. It demolished at a stroke the lawfulness of all government founded upon conquest. It swept away all the rubbish of accumulated centuries of servitude. It announced in a practical form to the world the transcendent truth of the unalienable sovereignty of the people. It proved that the social compact was no figment of the imagination; but a real solid and sacred bond of the social union [emphasis per original]."

Although an attack upon the educational foundations of this "nation conceived in liberty" is putting America to the ultimate test, there is reason for optimism. Secular radicals cannot extinguish the capacity of computer search engines, which disclose the truth about historic documents, such as the above quotation.

Commendable resources include *Understanding the Constitution* by David Gibbs Jr., and David Gibbs III, and WallBuilders.com, resourced by the historian David Barton. A special thank you goes to Phyllis

Schlafly, who has a superb background in the law, for her book, *The Supremacists: The Tyranny of Judges and How to Stop It*. Others to whom I am indebted, too numerous to place here, are listed in Appendix D: Citation Notes, with content that outlines their very important contributions.

Our well-founded hope is in the resurgence of readers who are banding together for political action because of their concerns for citizen knowledge.

It has been my privilege to chair a grand jury study on problems in higher education. This occurred at the time radicals were given tenure privileges, which gave them job security in public schools. This experience was an eye-opener. The Jury Presentment is included as Appendix A. Also, American history has been a constant companion throughout our family's history, which began in America with Nicholas Norris in 1654. Several family members served in the war for independence. At least one was at Valley Forge.

Endless thanks go to my dear wife Carlene, whose love and encouragement are of inestimable value. Finally, I am grateful for our gifted daughters, Sharon Thompson and Sara Skinner, who were helpful in writing this book.

Introduction:
Reality

From the beginning, Judeo-Christian principles have been the foundation for American public dialogue and government policy. They serve as the solid basis for political activism in support of a better socioeconomic environment. Found in American homes, truth from the Hebrew Christian Bible has enabled individual liberty to prevail over secular empires because it is a practical message about reality from man's Creator.

In their quest for liberty, Americans focused upon the conspicuously self-evident "Laws of Nature and of Nature's God." It is the governing character of these principles (laws), such as humility, the Golden Rule, and the Ten Commandments, that leads to success. This is the sure foundation upon which man's right to "life, liberty, and the pursuit of happiness" rests. Called "virtue" by America's Founding Fathers, the impartial and divine element frees man to do what is right. "Where the Spirit of the Lord is, there is liberty" (2 Cor. 3:17).

Word of the God of creation and creation's nature has strangely disappeared from the lexicon of public education. Ideas for decision making have one of two origins—either materialistic and mortal or a basis upon reality of everlasting truth, according to God's design. William Blackstone's *Commentaries on the Laws of England* were used by Abraham Lincoln and continued to be used by students of the law into the 1920s. Blackstone said: "Man, considered as a creature, must necessarily be subject to the laws [principles] of his Creator ... These laws laid down by God are the eternal immutable laws of good

1

and evil … This law of nature dictated by God himself, is of course superior in obligation to any other. It is binding over the entire globe, in all countries, and at all times: no human laws are of any validity if contrary to this."[1]

Knowledge of the Bible, the Great Reformation (1517-1648), and the American experience inspires individuals to become self-governing and, on a broader scale, inspires communities and the nation as a whole to overcome the tyranny of moral confusion. Even the German atheist Friedrich Nietzsche understood the source of freedom for his way of life when he wrote: "Remove Christianity and the ideas fall too."[2]

First Principle
The God of Creation Is Man's Benefactor.

That the God of creation is man's benefactor is so foundational it cannot be arrived at by any other proposition. It is the basic principle upon which all other principles follow. When man chooses to walk according to God's benevolent law, he learns of the power that is God's alone and by which God grants him victory over evil. This reality about creation's nature reveals God's protection. The following are two examples that illustrate this reality.

In the middle of a hillside surrounded by beautiful homes was a swampland that absorbed the surface water coming down from the properties above. This swampy area was filled with dirt and resulted in serious flooding below it. The goal of the neighbors living below was to solve the problem without an expensive lawsuit. The developer of the swampland was confronted with the truth. Knowing the historic consequences of rejecting truth, the developer agreed with reality. At considerable expense, he kindly provided a large trench to collect and reroute the water away from the development. His acknowledgment of the timeless laws of creation's nature caused him to solve the problem and avoid the consequences that come when truth is rejected. Policies consistent with the truth provide significant benefits for states and nations as well.

Conversely, those who persist in the fantasy of revisionist morality (moral relativism) and a central government that compromises the people's right to be fully informed have, in fact, ignored the irreversible laws of creation's nature. When liberal majorities on the Supreme Court and secular educators fail to uphold the God-honoring predicate of the *US Constitution*, they are, in effect, empowering atheistic revisionism that preys on societies. At a United Nations forum, December 7, 1988, Mikhail Gorbachev, atheist leader of the Soviet Union, repudiated the atheistic dogma shared by Karl Marx and Charles Darwin. Reflecting upon the disintegration of the secular (progressive) system, Gorbachev said: "The compelling necessity of the principle of freedom of choice is … clear to us. The failure to recognize this … is fraught with very dire consequences…. Freedom of choice is a universal principle to which there should be no exceptions. We have not come to the conclusion of the immutability of this principle simply through good motives. We have been led to it through impartial analysis of the objective processes of our time. This objective fact presupposes respect for other people's views."[3] He instituted glasnost, which allowed the people to be informed and free to communicate.*

Whether or not Gorbachev realized it, the Soviet empire was being forced to acknowledge that those who reject the "sovereignty of man under God over government" run into the immutable laws of creation's nature. Those laws support life, liberty, and the pursuit of happiness. In contrast, the vacillating laws of man lead to exploitation, cultural decay,

---

*   Failure to acknowledge the benevolent laws of God and creation's nature and conform to moral truth guarantees harmful consequences. Mikhail Gorbachev, leader of the Soviet Union from 1985 to 1991, tried to prevent its collapse by relaxing socialistic rule. To do this, he adopted perestroika and glasnost including property rights, but socialism had gone too far. Beginning in 1989, the puppet Communist governments in captive countries controlled by the Soviets were overthrown by the people. The Soviet Union fell apart when captive countries quit sending them the revenue required to keep the socialist economy going. Writing of perestroika, Gorbachev's wife Raisa said: "Our society has set out on the path of renewal and of demolishing totalitarianism and the obsolete command system of administering the country" (Raisa Gorbachev, *Reminiscences and Reflections*, Harper Collins, 1991, p. 174). See "Appendix C, "How Socialism Exploits Mankind …," Part IV—Supplemental Material, in this book.

poverty, and tyranny. When God's benevolent provision is rejected in any particular, the rejecter bears the price of that sin against himself and the will of God. A most insightful analysis has been presented by Marvin Olasky. As a Marxist intellectual, he was very highly regarded by the chairman of his PhD academic program and dissertation committee at the University of Michigan. Marvin Olasky, who became disillusioned by the shallowness of socialistic panaceas, became a solid convert to Christianity.[4] Olasky concurs with Whittaker Chambers, who came to believe in God after being a Communist Party member in the 1920s and 1930s. In the autobiography *Witness,* Whittaker Chambers writes: "A Communist breaks because he must choose at last between irreconcilable opposites—God or man, Soul [conscience] or Mind [emotions], Freedom or Communism.... The crisis of the Western world exists to the degree in which it is indifferent to God."

It is necessary to reestablish the meaning of some key words in this study. This is because of the persistent dishonesty of radicals who migrated into the soft sciences** of universities and public schools saddled by tenure guarantees (which crept silently into collective bargaining laws starting in the early 1970s).

"Old European secular philosophy" is a general term that includes the many sects championed by the God-rejecting intellectuals in Europe. The traditional American use of the word "secular" is different. The American use of the term refers to government and other activities that are not in themselves religious, but are directed within a greater context that respects the values and will of God.

The word "secular" was used in America to distinguish national, state, and local governments from church governments. This has become too confusing for modern-day use on two counts. First, used by radicals, the word "secular" leaves people blindsided to the fact that the science of their agenda is driven by deception and insistence on an atheistic-secular worldview monopoly. Secondly, their atheistic worldview is religious,

---

** The soft sciences include literature, journalism, education strategies, political science, life-origins biology, life-origins geology, history, law studies, religion, social studies, arts, psychology, and ecology.

4

with a deeply held Darwinian view about the origin and meaning of life. In 1961, the Supreme Court in *Torcaso v. Watkins* classified secular humanism (the title used by secular militants in academia) as a religion. To avoid the misleading use of the word "secular," we suggest there are times that the phrase **atheistic-secular be used**. Instead of being secular authoritarian based, the American predicate for determining public policy is impartial, higher-authority morality-based.

American conservatism transcends both the good and evil intentions of today's adherents to the old European secular philosophy—the religious and political left. **Revisionist morality, supported by the Darwinian theory for life's origin, meaning, and purpose, represents one of the greatest evils of our time.***** In this book, the focus upon the danger to American liberty has been narrowed to those who are at the seat of the problem—secular militants.

In fact, the American states did not become united until the constitutional delegates agreed to amendments that were specific about religious and educational freedom from government and nongovernment dictation. The first ten amendments included the codification of the principles outlined in the *Declaration of Independence* (separation from authoritarian rule). **Far from being secular, all aspects of human endeavor, including government, fall under the purview of creation's God. The value system for determining the proper role of laws and the use of government power is clear.** We ought to obey God rather than men (Acts 5:29). Adoption of this morally-specific, nonsectarian, God-honoring predicate has served as a marvelous unifier for our diverse immigrant nation.

As Justice Brandeis said, "Sunlight is the best disinfectant." We no

---

*** Charles Darwin published his theory for a God-rejecting worldview in the book *The Origin of Species,* published in 1859. There is some adaptation within species, but the Herculean efforts of science pretenders to find evolution between species fail. Sir Arthur Keith, a leading evolutionist has written: "Evolution is unproved and unprovable. We believe it only because the only alternative is special creation which is unthinkable" -Sir Arthur Keith, *as citation* in Wallie A. Criswell's *Did Man Just Happen?* (Grand Rapids MI: Zondervan, 1972), 73). D. M. S. Watson acknowledged the same in *Nature,* vol. 124, August 10, 1929, pp. 231–234).

longer have public education. In the behavioral and political sciences it has become government education comparable to the monopoly state doctrine that decimated Medieval Europe. The secular militants claim to be patriots because, as they say, dissent is American. What they mean is evident from how they have gutted traditional American values in public education. They demand freedom for themselves but reject the American concept of academic freedom (the freedom to be honestly informed) and the freedom of others to make their own choices. The soft underbelly of the secular left is the fact that they cannot withstand the competition of ideas. For them, it is intolerable to allow students to learn of the God of creation alongside their atheistic lifeview.

An elaboration of "In God We Trust" is found in Proverbs 3:5–6: "Trust in the LORD with all thine heart; and lean not unto thine own understanding. In all thy ways acknowledge him, and he shall direct thy paths."

The "In God We Trust" worldview has been the foundation for public education, beginning in the original thirteen colonies and continuing for over 250 years. The Supreme Court's ruling in the *Everson v. Board of Education* decision of 1947 began a dramatic shift away from "In God We Trust." See Chapter 6 for details on this Supreme Court ruling. We review the civic religion adopted by immigrants from around the world in Chapters 1 through 4 and Part IV, Appendix B, the *Iowa Bill of Rights,* taken in part from the *Declaration of Independence.* The strategy for restoring competition in education and choice by the people is outlined in Chapters 11 and 12.

The unionization of teachers and accompanying tenure law have enabled a small cadre of radicals to enforce their attacks against God in education. The conservative historian and former Speaker of the United States House of Representatives Newt Gingrich stated: "Those who want absolute proof you cannot teach American history honestly and accurately without reference to God, go to the Lincoln Memorial and read where in Lincoln's second inaugural, March 1865, he referred to God fourteen times and used two quotes from the Bible.

Lincoln Memorial Statue

There are millions of honest hardworking teachers, but they have no more control over the lifeview being taught in the soft sciences than do parents. An entirely different system for educating American youth is needed that will bypass the leftist teachers' union monopoly; the education tax must be routed through the parents, similar to the G.I. Bill following World War II. This bill provided that education sought by veterans be paid from taxpayer revenues, and the veterans had the freedom to use the tuition grant in a public or private institution of their choice.

There are three achievements of secular progressives that have enabled leftists to control behavioral instruction in public schools (see Chapters 7 through 9). Their first big achievement was the counterrevolution advanced by secular majorities on the Supreme Court. Leftists' opposition to American traditions and conventional morality intended by the *US Constitution* is illustrated by the *Everson v. Board of Education* decision. Second was the takeover, beginning in the 1960s, of the then-conservative National Education Association by leftist militants (see Chapters 7 through 10). Also in the 1960s, secular progressives, committed to the elimination of self-government and liberty, reached their third achievement—the unionization of government teachers.

A government-established union monopoly, like an established state church, undermines the people's right to choose between providers that must compete for a following. Union monopolies have always been power-corrupting institutions. Whatever their agenda by subject or region, accountability to competition is removed and evil prevails. Union monopolies are antithetical to government of, by, and for the people. It is the collective political power foolishly granted to autoworker unions that brought the American auto industry to its knees. It is the collective political advantage of unionism that makes it possible for radicals to impose their atheistic worldview over the objections of both the majority of parents and the millions of excellent teachers caught in the union web. Consistent violation of citizen authority (government by, for, and of the people) is the radical politics of fascism—authoritarian hierarchical government. The definition of Fascism applied here is the politics of authoritarians who by any means prevent the citizens from exercising control over the use of government power through like-minded representatives.

Detailed in Chapter 7, the loss of citizen control over what our nation's youth are taught in the behavioral studies hinges on two teachers' tenure contract paragraphs demanded by union bosses when negotiating with local school boards. The first devastating paragraph provides teacher tenure guarantees that supersede the authority of school administrators to replace employees. The second harmful paragraph makes it a crime to disclose bad teacher performance to the public or to other schools that are considering hiring the teacher until costly and lengthy legal proceedings have approved such disclosure.

Professionals like medical doctors, engineers, plumbers, and airline pilots—vital to our society—do not have tenure guarantees. Yet what is being taught to America's youth is of even greater importance.

Some repetition has been used for emphasis and to tie the chapters together.

Benjamin Franklin

Benjamin Franklin, a delegate from Pennsylvania to the second Continental Congress and signer of the *Constitution of the United States*, wrote about the First Principle in his *Articles of Belief*: "I believe there is one supreme, most perfect Being ... Also when I stretch my imagination through and beyond our system of planets, beyond the visible fixed stars themselves, into that space that is [in] every way infinite, and conceive it filled with suns like ours, each with a chorus of worlds forever moving round him; then this little ball on which we move, seems, even in my narrow imagination, to be almost nothing, and myself less than nothing, and of no sort of consequence ... That I may be preserved from atheism ... Help me, O Father!... For all thy innumerable benefits; for life, and reason ... My good God, I thank thee!"[5]

Is it too late for America? Not at all.

PART I:
Government

Chapters 1 to 6

"Although all men are born free, and all nations might be so, yet too true it is, that slavery has been the general lot of the human race. Ignorant—they have been cheated; asleep—they have been surprised; divided—the yoke has been forced upon them. But what is the lesson? That because the people may betray themselves, they ought to give themselves up, blindfold, to those who have an interest in betraying

James Madison

them? Rather conclude that the people ought to be enlightened, to be awakened, to be united."

James Madison, Essay: Who Are the Keepers of the People's Liberties? Madison served as the fourth president of the United States (1809–1817) and is considered the principal author of the United States Constitution. *In 1788, he wrote over a third of the Federalist Papers, still the most influential commentary on the* Constitution. *Madison was responsible for writing the first ten amendments to the* Constitution, *also known as the* Bill of Rights.

CHAPTER 1
Immortal Principles Central to Liberty and American Greatness

What is the common bond that enabled Americans to establish the greatest nation on earth? The *USA Today*/Gallup Poll published May 6, 2010, reports that 92 percent of Americans believe in God and only 5 percent said they oppose the National Day of Prayer. The problem is that public schools stopped teaching how the basic American belief "In God We Trust" translates into principles for political decisions that made America the overwhelming choice of immigrants from around the world.

Having confronted the barriers to success imposed by the British Crown at the First Continental Congress, the Founding Fathers needed to address the following questions:

I.   How do we bring into focus the justification for independence that can, in fact, support the life, liberty, and happiness that the colonists found possible?

II. How do we declare the sovereignty of man under God over government, upon which respect for impartial law, citizen self-rule, and liberty is justified?

III. How do we emphasize the need for strict separation from the British king and other pretender gods, who have managed to betray and exploit mankind down through history?

IV. What must we proclaim that will convince other nations to have confidence in the United States as a sovereign entity?

The answers to these questions became the basis for the unique principles for government in America. The *Declaration of Independence* provided a moral and just basis for law as no other document before or since. These principles were adopted unanimously by the Second Continental Congress on July 2, 1776. On July 4, 1776, the delegates signed their names to the *Declaration*, and the new nation—independent from Great Britain—was born.

The people of England were not the issue. Americans were fond of the people and valued their trade relationships. At issue was limiting the oppressive ways of British government and the need for tough-minded rejection of practices that violated liberty and citizen incentive to be self-governing.

John Adams

On July 3, John Adams, a delegate to the Continental Congress from Massachusetts who later served as the second president of the United States, wrote the following to his wife Abigail: "The second day of July 1776 will be the most memorable epoch in the history of America. I am apt to believe that it will be celebrated by succeeding generations as the great anniversary festival. It ought to be commemorated as the Day of Deliverance by solemn acts of devotion to God Almighty. It ought to be solemnized with pomp and parade, with shows, games, sports, guns, bells, bonfires, and illuminations from one end of this continent to the other from this time forward forever more" (cited by David McCullough, *John Adams*, New York: Simon & Schuster Paperbacks, 2001, 130).

On July 8, 1776, the *Declaration* was read in public for the first time, outside Independence Hall in Philadelphia, accompanied by the ringing of the Liberty Bell. On August 2, 1776, the members of Congress signed the parchment copy. It provides the logic and justification for the chain of authority described by Hamilton Abert Long as "man under God over government" (www.archives.gov/exhibits/charters/declaration_history.html).

A Definite, Unique, American Belief
Translated Into Specific Principles
for Governments Does Exist

James Wilson was one of six men who signed the *Declaration of Independence* and the *Constitution of the United States.* His contribution to the deliberations of the *Constitution* was second only to James Madison's. Addressing the Pennsylvania Ratifying Convention for the new constitution, Wilson stated: "I beg to read a few words from the *Declaration of Independence* made by the representatives of the United States and recognized by the whole Union:

James Wilson

"We hold these truths to be self-evident, that all men are created equal, that they are endowed by their Creator with certain unalienable Rights, that among these are Life, Liberty and the pursuit of Happiness. — That to secure these rights, Governments are instituted among Men, deriving their just powers from the consent of the governed, — That whenever any Form of Government becomes destructive of these ends, it is the Right of the People to alter or to abolish it, and to institute new Government, laying its foundation on such principles and organizing its powers in such form, as to them shall seem most likely to effect their Safety and Happiness."

Wilson concluded, "This [*Declaration*] is the broad basis on which our independence [from authoritarian rule] was placed; on the same certain and solid foundation this [the *Constitution of the United States*] system is erected" (cited in John Elliot, *Elliot's Debates, The Debates In The Several State Conventions Adoption Of The Federal Constitution*, Philadelphia, Pennsylvania 11-20-1787, Book I, published 1836, 457).

The American Principles rest on the *First Principle* (emphasized in the Introduction). Compromise of any of the following principles leads to very harmful consequences.

American Principle One

The Spiritual Nature of Man Is Supreme

"All men are created ... endowed by their Creator ..."
Declaration of Independence

Foundational to liberty and the American approach to government is the fact that man is of divine origin. His spiritual or God-honoring religious nature is held as being of supreme importance. Upholding man's God-given "rights" from abuses sanctioned by governments makes liberty possible. The divine quality of these rights calls for the unequivocal rejection of the authoritarian entitlements claimed by elitists of all stripes—kings, authoritarian politicians, clergy, educators, and militarists. This principle enshrines certain limits that must, for the sake of liberty, be placed upon the use of the law and government power.

Humble support for the sovereignty of man under God over government is the guarantor of freedom for family wholeness, the right to choose, self-reliance, and prosperity. People who know the truth can reject, without fear, the alarming chatter of atheistic sectarians.

American Principle Two

God Is the Source of Unalienable Rights

"All men are ... **endowed by their Creator** with certain
unalienable Rights, that among these are Life, Liberty,
and the pursuit of Happiness."
Declaration of Independence

"*We The People Of The State Of Iowa*, grateful
to the Supreme Being for the blessings hitherto enjoyed, and
feeling our dependence on Him for a continuation of those
blessings, do ordain and establish a free and independent
government, by the name of the State of Iowa ..."
Preamble, Constitution of Iowa, adopted in 1846—
seventy years after the *Declaration of Independence*

Education that does not emphasize that man's unalienable rights are the gift of God is energizing the enemies of the family, self-rule, prosperity, and liberty.

Belief in a Higher Authority holds that man does not originate law. Legislators articulate pre-existing law and give it particular applications to changing circumstances. Americans' progress in handling changing circumstances is testimony to the universality and timeless nature of the principle, "God Is the Source of Unalienable Rights." Alexander Hamilton, in *The Federalist*, No. 78, says: "A constitution is, in fact, and must be regarded by the judges, as a fundamental law." When a particular statute violates the meaning of the *Constitution,* it is the duty of judicial tribunals to disregard it and adhere to the *Constitution*. Those who reject God's authority and proceed to fix the rights of others are by definition false gods and in practice become tyrants.

During the 1765 crisis caused by the king's Stamp Act, John Adams, when writing the *Dissertation on the Canon and Feudal Law*, August 12, 1765, the *Boston Gazette,* pointed out that liberty was not man's creation or something radically new to the world, but rights "derived from our Maker," rights "indisputable, unalienable," "inherent," "essential," "divine," and even acknowledged since the Middle Ages by British law.

"The sacred Rights of mankind are not to be rummaged from among old parchments or musty records. They are written, as with a sunbeam, in the whole volume of human nature, by the Hand of the Divinity itself, and can never be erased or voided or obscured by mortal power" (teachingamericanhistory.org › ... › Alexander Hamilton *The Farmer Refuted*, 1775).

"We further recommend the most clear and explicit assertion and vindication of our rights and liberties to be entered on the public records, that the world may know, in present and all future generations, that we have a clear knowledge and a just sense of them, and, with submission to Divine Providence that we never can be slaves" (John Adams, adopted on October 14, 1765, by the town meeting of Braintree, Massachusetts, and sent to their representatives in the Massachusetts state legislature).

American Principle Three

Upholding the Traditional Family Is Paramount

**"laying its foundation on such principles
and organizing its powers
in such form, as to them shall seem
most likely to effect their Safety and Happiness."**
Declaration of Independence

Protecting the traditional family as a distinct institution is among the highest priorities for a nation's laws. This historic arrangement has proven overwhelmingly to be the best setting for raising children to live healthy, responsible, and productive lives (Gen. 2:23–24).

"That government is instituted and ought to be exercised for the benefit of the people; which consists in the enjoyment of life and liberty, and generally of pursuing and obtaining happiness and safety" (James Madison in the first session of the US Congress, proposing the Bill of Rights amendments be added to the Constitution of the United States).

"The most important consequence of marriage is, that the husband and the wife become in law only one person" (James Wilson, *Natural Rights of Marriage*, 1792, teachingamericanhistory.org).

American Principle Four

All Men Are Equal
In the Sight of God and the Law

"that all men are created equal ..."
Declaration of Independence

People of different faiths, with different racial and cultural backgrounds, and people who are gifted in different ways are created equal at birth and deserve to be treated equally by the civil and criminal justice systems. Any concept of authoritarianism that presumes to override the sovereignty of man under God over government is a violation of "equal in the sight of God and the law."

"The multitude I am speaking of is the body of people—no contemptible multitude—for whose sake government is instituted; or rather, who have themselves erected it, solely for their own good—to whom even kings and all in subordination to them, are strictly speaking, servants and not masters" (Samuel Adams, essay in the *Boston Gazette*, 1771).

American Principle Five

Liberty—from Oppression by Big Government
and Nongovernment Authoritarians—Is Vital

**"unalienable Rights,
that among these are ... liberty."**
Declaration of Independence

"Liberty and life are the gratuitous gifts of heaven. I shall certainly be excused from adducing any formal arguments to evince, that life, and whatever is necessary for the safest of life, are the natural rights of man. Some things are so difficult; others are so plain, that they cannot be proved" (Supreme Court Justice James Wilson, *Lectures*, delivered in the College of Philadelphia 1790-1791. Volume II, Part II, Chapter 1, *Lorenzo Press*, 1804).

Liberty and self-reliance for independence are God's gifts for man to claim. Liberty in the context of the *Declaration of Independence* and Preamble to the *Constitution* means freedom from government activity that would undermine the development of citizen self-reliance. Accepting promises of politicians who use the public treasury to provide things that replace personal responsibility is a trap. Paternalistic government services attract and enlarge an irresponsible voting block, that when reduced to dependence, cannot be reversed. Helping those who are incapable for reasons beyond their control is, of course, man's duty and beneficial to all.

"And can the liberties of a nation be thought secure when we have removed their only firm basis, a conviction in the minds of the people that these liberties are a gift of God? That they are not violated but with His wrath? Indeed I tremble for my country when I reflect that God is just: that His justice cannot sleep forever" (Thomas Jefferson: signer and principal author of the *Declaration of Independence* and third president of the United States, Notes on Virginia Q.XVIII, 1782. ME 2:227).

American Principle Six

The Written *Constitution* Established
by Americans Is a Tool for Governing

**Governments derive "their just powers
from the consent of the governed."**
Declaration of Independence

Americans established government when covenanting to share a small portion of their God-given rights to use force and keep thieves out of the corncrib. It is the tax revenues provided by the people that give government its power.

The tool is to be used in ways to achieve the goals spelled out philosophically in the Preamble: *"We the People* of the United States, in Order to form a more perfect Union, establish Justice, insure domestic Tranquility, provide for the common defense, promote the general Welfare, [**meaning common needs that do not conflict with or hamper the development of the work ethic and personal self-reliance**] and secure the Blessings of Liberty to ourselves and our Posterity, do ordain and establish this *Constitution for the United States of America."*

We, the people, have as our guide God-honoring principles for directing the use of the government power. When, during the Civil War, Abraham Lincoln dedicated the field where thousands gave their lives at Gettysburg, he concluded, "that this nation, under God, shall have a new birth of freedom—and that government of the people, by the people, for the people, shall not perish from the earth" (The Gettysburg Address, Gettysburg, Pennsylvania, November 19, 1863).

Some delegates to the Constitutional Convention believed these principles of the *Declaration of Independence* for guiding government action would prevail without amending the *Constitution* because many states had already adopted a *Bill of Rights*. Obviously the delegates did not anticipate the pervasiveness of the federal judiciary as it has since developed. Ultimately the Founding Fathers at the state level made a most significant contribution by insisting that the nation's *Constitution* be amended by a *Bill of Rights*.

The principles of the *Declaration* were expanded and codified, then added as amendments to the federal *Constitution*. An example of the carryover of the *Declaration* many years later is the *Bill of Rights* in the *Constitution of the new State of Iowa*, Part IV, Appendix B.

American Principle Seven

The Moral Duties of Civility Are Also a Predicate
for Interpreting Constitutional Meaning

"We hold these truths to be self-evident ..."
Declaration of Independence

**"Tis substantially true that virtue or morality
is a necessary spring of popular government. Who
that is a sincere friend to it, can look with Indifference
upon attempts to shake the foundation of the fabric?"**
George Washington, Farewell Address

The impartial **"Laws of Nature and of Nature's God"**[****] are the moral connectors that uphold the work ethic, prosperity, and civil community. When we speak of morality here, we are speaking of what John Marshall wrote in the *Marbury v. Madison* opinion. He said, "The government of the United States has been emphatically termed a government of laws, and not of men" (www.quotecounterquote.com/.../government-of-laws-and-not-of-men-is.html). It is this bold rejection of the history of law determined by atheistic-secular authoritarians and the elevation of natural-law philosophy that caused immigrants, by countless millions, to come to America. And it is the ironclad benefits resulting from applying the impartial "Laws of Nature and of Nature's God" that cause them to stay in America.

The Founding Fathers wrote God-honoring natural-law philosophy into the *Declaration of Independence*. **Morality inherent in natural law**

[****] The phrase "Nature's God" used in the *Declaration of Independence* did not originate with Americans. The laws of nature's God include the biblical standards of morality. When the bond between God and man was broken in the Garden of Eden, the forces of evil that seek to defy creation's nature were unleashed. "The *law of nature* was a common term used by historic legal writers such as Grotius, Burlamaqui, Blackstone and others. The *law of nature's God*, a lesser used term, was more commonly called *the divine law*, or *the revealed law*" (*Loning Historical Reference Works*).

is the underpinning of the *Constitution*. Persistence in upholding this perspective separates the *Constitution* as a tool from defilement by the adherents of man-made law (Alexander Hamilton, *Tully Papers*, in Philadelphia newspapers 1794). Natural law reflects the common-sense separation of wrong from what is right, as does man's God-given conscience. In 2 Corinthians, Chapter 1, Paul rejoices in "the testimony of our conscience, that in simplicity and godly sincerity, not with fleshly wisdom, but by the grace of God, we have had our conversation in the world, and more abundantly to you-ward." Provisions that distinguish the application of American Constitutional law include not destroying innocent life, not stealing, and not being untruthful. Lying when a person gives evidence in a court of law is the crime of perjury. Liberal law professors avoid discussions about the origin of natural law because that requires an acknowledgement that the predicate for Constitutional interpretation—"government of laws, and not of men"—resides in higher biblical authority.

The natural-law philosophy underpinning of the American *Constitution* is in direct conflict with secular law, which leads to political adventurism, exploitation, death, and slavery. The secular law of **open-mindedness** required of teachers by Professor John Dewey is an evil education doctrine (John S. Brubacher and Willis Rudy, *Higher Education Transition*, New York: Harper and Row, 1958, 310). It blindsides students to the horrific differences between good and evil and causes them to go along with the pagan laws of man contrived by liberal judges, legislators, and educators. The atheistic-secular philosophy for law identifies with what the Solon of Athens described as "government by incalculable and changeable decrees" (Will and Ariel Durant, *The Story of Civilization, Vol. II, The Life of Greece*, Simon and Schuster, 1939, 118). This is an evil repudiation of the solid basis necessary for prosperity and undermines the self-government enablements of man, for which the *Constitution* was written.

The moral absolutes essential for laws to eliminate abuses or misunderstanding on the part of those hired to serve in government fit into two categories. **First** laws for the separation of powers within national, state, and local governments established by the *Constitution*

23

apart from the amendments that were added later. In this set of laws, the powers of the three branches of government are separated with function exclusivity to serve as a check against one another and to promote balanced enforcement. Adherence to this constitutional principle enables observers to see, expose, and remove those who have access to the people's treasury and are found to be authoritarian, dishonest, or thievish. The most important check is the secret ballot and power of the people to vote and remove from office those who misuse their authority.

The **second** category of laws resting on moral certainty follow the *Declaration of Independence* pattern for separation from hierarchical rule outlined in the *Bill of* [citizen] *Rights* that was added to the *Constitution*. These laws are intended to prevent government servants from perverting established law to grant rights to criminals that are harmful to the public or using the public's treasury to subsidize slothful citizens and thereby attract an irresponsible voting block. This category of laws is needed to protect a strong, responsible citizen majority—the survival of self-government and liberty from tyrannical government rule. **As long as judges do not use their independence to twist the meaning of the *Constitution* and the *Bill of Rights* to mask an authoritarian secular agenda, the American principles for life and liberty are not impaired or diminished.**

"Men are qualified for civil liberty in exact proportion to their disposition to put moral chains on their own appetites. Society cannot exist unless a controlling power upon will and appetite be placed somewhere … men of intemperate minds cannot be free. Their passions forge their fetters" (Edmund Burke, British supporter of the American Revolution, November 3, 1774, speech to the electors of Bristol, England, quoted by Hillsdale College *Imprimis* Vol. 20, No. 9).

"Liberty and security in government depend not on the limits, which the rulers may please to assign to the exercise of their own powers, but on the boundaries, within which their powers are circumscribed by the *Constitution*. With us, the powers of magistrates, call them by whatever name you please, are the grants of the people … The supreme power is in them [the people]; and in them, even when the *Constitution* is formed, and government is in operation, the supreme power still remains. A portion of their authority they, indeed, delegate; but they delegate that portion in whatever manner, in whatever measure, for whatever time, to whatever persons, and on whatever conditions they choose to fix" (US Supreme Court Justice James Wilson, *Lectures*, 1790–1791).

The limited purpose for judicial independence is to enable judges to settle disputes without being pressured by special interests. When judges establish policies by legislating or administrating, they have seriously violated their jurisdiction and become fascistic. That is, they are overriding and preventing the people as sovereigns whose exclusive authority it is to elect like-minded representatives to do the legislating and serve as administrators. Judges do have the duty to alert citizen sovereigns about a perceived need for legislation. That is covered in Chapter 6.

"The great object of my fear is the federal judiciary. That body, like gravity, ever acting, with noiseless foot, and unalarming advance, gaining ground step by step, and holding what it gains, is engulfing insidiously the special governments into the jaws of that which feeds them" (Thomas Jefferson, letter to Judge Spencer Roane, Mar 9, 1821, www.marksquotes.com/Founding-Fathers/Jefferson/index7.htm).

Violations of the principle that the moral duties of civility are a predicate for interpreting the meaning of the *Constitution* have unleashed functional disorder and are doing great harm to society in America. Upholding the intent and meaning of "certain unalienable [supreme] rights" of the people, outlined in the *Declaration of Independence* and the *Bill of Rights,* is indispensable. Laws that protect sodomy, same-sex marriage, abortion, and the privilege of teacher tenure guarantees are a violation of vital American principles that protect the public from exposure to unsavory and virulent evil practices. When judges are appointed who add harmful practices as a law-protected right, they undermine the right to life and liberty and even do harm to the economy. All citizens, including judges, have the **duty to protect the unalienable God-given rights to life and responsible use of liberty for others.**

American Principle Eight

The Overriding Concern When Writing the Constitution
Was Imposing a Check on Man's Sin-Prone Behavior

"He [the authoritarian] **has combined with others to subject
us jurisdiction** [control] **foreign to our *Constitution*
and unacknowledged by our laws, giving
his assent to their acts of pretended legislation."**
Declaration of Independence

Man has a selfish nature, and those who achieve power tend to abuseit. Frederic Bastiat in *The Law* and Charles Spurgeon both lamented the sinful nature that causes man to believe that he has the right to rule over others. Bastiat addressed the need for laws that would curtail this supremacist impulse while at the same time preserving individual liberty. Spurgeon deplored both Catholic and Protestant hierarchies that seek to micromanage the people and local leaders by controlling their resources and dictating their agenda.

James Madison wrote, "The only distinction between freedom and slavery consists of this: in the former state, man is governed by laws to which he has given his consent, either in person or, by his representative: In the latter he is governed by the will of another.... If men were angels, no government would be necessary" (cited by Forrest McDonald, *The Intellectual Origins of the Constitution*, Lawrence, Kansas, University of Kansas Press, 1985, pp. 160 and 205 respectively).

It is the evil ways of men that make this a dangerous world that requires freedom-loving individuals to be tough-minded. It is a tough-minded refusal to compromise and negotiate away the timeless principles briefed in the *Declaration* that sends the enemy down losers' lane.

American Principle Nine

Authoritarians in Government Are a Parasitic
and Ever-Present Danger

**"Taking away our charters, Abolishing our
most valuable laws, and altering fundamentally
the forms of our governments** [constitutions]."
Declaration of Independence

"The spirit of encroachment tends to consolidate the powers of all the departments in one, and thus to create, whatever the form of government, a real despotism. A just estimate of that love of power, and proneness to abuse it, which predominates in the human heart, is sufficient to satisfy us of the truth of this position" (President George Washington's *Farewell Address,* www.liberty1.org/farewell.htm).

Two notable efforts by power-hungry authoritarians occurred near the end of the war for independence. First, army officers were conspiring to take control of Congress. Second was an effort to make George Washington king. He squashed both of them abruptly. After all, Americans had just been through a bloody war with England to get rid of rule by authoritarians, religious and secular.

An axiom for detecting the corrupt and evil use of power is to follow the flow of money to politicians inside and outside of government. Chief among tactics for overriding the will of the people at the state and local levels is bad election finance law. The importation of millions of campaign dollars from homosexual- and abortion-rights advocates from outside a region to fund the campaigns of radicals in the region to be represented is destructive of representative government. This should be prohibited.

"In questions of power then, let no more be heard of confidence in man, but bind him down from mischief by the chains of the *Constitution*" (Thomas Jefferson: Draft Kentucky Resolutions, 1798. ME 17:388).

American Principle Ten

Government Must Be Decentralized

**"repeated injuries and usurpations, all having in
direct object the establishment of an absolute
Tyranny** [British King] **over these States."**
Declaration of Independence

The American system is "a Republic—a federation, or combination, of
central and state republics—under which: the different governments will
control each other.… Within each republic there are two safeguarding
features: (a) a division of powers, as well as (b) a system of checks and
balances between separate departments: hence a double security arises
[essential] to the rights of the people" (*Federalist*, No. 51, by James
Madison).

Regarding the federal government usurping essential citizen rights,
"True barriers [for] of our liberty are our State governments" (President
Thomas Jefferson's First Inaugural Address (www.bartley.com/124/
pres16.html).

"The necessity of reciprocal checks in the exercise of political power, by
dividing and distributing it into different depositories, and constituting
each the guardian of the public weal against invasions by the others, has
been evinced by experiments ancient and modern; some of them in our
country and under our own eyes. To preserve them must be as necessary
as to institute them" (George Washington's Farewell Address).

"Bear in mind this sacred principle, that though the will of the majority
is in all cases to prevail, that will to be rightful must be reasonable; that
the minority possesses their equal rights, which equal laws must protect,
and to violate would be oppression" (President Thomas Jefferson's First
Inaugural Address).

Officials who bypass the principles of limited government are suppressing the supreme right of the people to rule. Such officials have violated their duties as trustees and are in effect usurpers, oppressors, and tyrants.

American Principle Eleven

Government and Union Monopolies
Involving Education or Religion Are
Prohibited—For Liberty's Sake

**"Congress shall make no law respecting an establishment
of religion, or prohibiting the free exercise thereof;
or abridging the freedom of speech, or of the press;
or the right of the people peaceably to assemble, and to
petition the Government for a 'redress of grievances.'"**
Constitution of the United States

Education that does not teach the timeless principles recorded in the *Declaration of Independence* **empowers the enemies of life and liberty for the pursuit of happiness**. The delegates to the Constitutional Convention understood this, and they focused upon the fact that governments are by nature a nesting place for tyrants of the mind.

With the tactics used by state-church monopolies, tenured secular authoritarians achieved control of the curriculum used in the soft sciences and the study of law taught in government schools. The weapons used by tenured radicals to enforce what must be taught include the ridicule and denigration of the reputation of anyone who dares to challenge leftist political correctness. The use of the word "science" is code for their atheistic human origins, meaning, and purpose dogma; "diversity" is code for demanding the approval of evil life practices; and "social justice" is code for using government power to force the transfer of wealth from the thrifty to their voting block. It is the collective political power granted to monopoly teacher unions and the establishment of tenure laws that empower the enemies of the family, human dignity, and self-government.

It is the competition of education suppliers that reduces inefficiencies in government-run schools and helps restrain moral pollution by tenured government radicals. The debasement of morality evident in the tragic church-state monopoly of Medieval Europe compares with the moral decline that started with government establishment of teacher unions.

The indispensable role of education and religious liberty in the preservation of American principles for government is "self-evident." Education that leaves new generations thinking of government as some vague entity leaves them confused about the truth and easy prey for manipulation by what Jefferson called "tyrants of the mind." Definite and specific American principles for government of a responsible nature do exist. Fifteen of them are the focus of this chapter. Education worthy of the name will emphasize that government is the servant of and for the people, the sovereigns under creation's God.

First-amendment law intended to prevent the suppression of the right of parents to choose between competing education suppliers for their children's education **are superior to all other laws—national, state, and local.**

American Principle Twelve

Vital to the American Work Ethic,
Property Ownership Must Be Secure

"are entitled to life, liberty and property ..."
Declaration, First Continental Congress, 1774

**"All men ... are endowed by their Creator
with certain unalienable Rights, that among these
are Life, Liberty and the pursuit of Happiness."**
Declaration of Independence

"That all men ... have certain inherent rights ... namely, the enjoyment of life and liberty, with the means of acquiring and possessing property" (*Virginia Declaration of Rights*, 1776).

"For even when we were with you, this we commanded you, that if any would not work, neither should he eat. For we hear that there are some which walk among you disorderly, working not at all, but are busybodies" (2 Thess. 3:10–11).

The emotionally charged appeal for the redistribution of the fruits of man's labor popularized later by Karl Marx (1818–83) as "each according to his ability, to each according to need" had been tried in the Plymouth Colony. Following extensive food shortages, Governor Bradford turned to the Bible for wisdom and then announced that settlers would have a plot of land, and thereafter be entitled to the fruits of their own labor (April, 1623). Entire families went to work, and hard times changed to a plentiful supply of food (www.bartleby.com/124/pres16.html).

Linking the work ethic to property ownership was a monumental break from the world's political history. The incentive of property ownership is the engine that makes an economy flourish. It is the value created in the usefulness of products provided by the worker suppliers that leads the buyer to spend his money to own the product.

American Principle Thirteen

Government Power and Taxes
Must Be Limited for Liberty's Sake

"imposing Taxes on us without our Consent ..."
Declaration of Independence

Low taxes and limited government are indispensable supports for property ownership and liberty. "He [the king] has erected a multitude of New Offices, and sent hither swarms of officers to harass our people, and eat out their substance" (*Declaration of Independence*).

Alexander Hamilton, in the *Federalist* No. 17, www.constitution.org/fed/federa17.htm, emphasizes that taxes should not be imposed at the federal level that enable the government to do things that go beyond the enumerated powers of the federal government and thereby take money from the people that should be available for state and local government needs (in effect, enabling federal usurpers to prevent government closest to the people). The Tenth Amendment was ratified on December 15, 1791. It restates the *Constitution*'s principle of federalism by providing that powers not granted to the national government or prohibited to the states are reserved to the states or to the people.

The *Federalist* No. 10, written by James Madison, condemned taxing the thrifty and financially independent citizens for purposes of leveling. He condemned this practice advanced by old European secular philosophy as "improper" and "wicked" (http://thomas.loc.gov/home/histdox/fed_10.htm).

Government debt that exceeds income cripples nations in the same devastating way that it cripples individuals, families, and corporations. "Indeed, we cannot too often inculcate upon you our desires, that all extraordinary grants and expensive measures may, upon all occasions, as much as possible, be avoided. The public money of this country is the toil and labor of the people …" (written by representatives of the town of Braintree, Massachusetts, to their legislative representative, *Braintree Records* 1765–66).

American Principle Fourteen

Life and Happiness Are Humanity's Goals

"Unalienable rights, that among these are Life,
… and the **pursuit of Happiness**."
Declaration of Independence

"Kings or parliaments could not give the rights essential to happiness … We claim them from a higher source—from the King of kings, and Lord of all the earth. They are not annexed to us by parchments and seals. They are created in us by the decrees of Providence … It would be an insult on the Divine Majesty to say that He has given or allowed any man or body of men a right to make me miserable. If no man or body of men has such a right, I have a right to be happy. If there can be no happiness without freedom, I have a right to be thus secured" (John Dickinson, reply to a Committee in Barbados, 1766, *Quotes By John Dickinson*).

"The consequence is, that happiness of society is the first law of every government. The people have a right to insist that this rule be observed; and are entitled to demand a moral security that the legislature will observe it. If they have not the first right, they are slaves; if they have not the second right [moral security], they are, every moment, exposed to slavery" (US Supreme Court Justice James Wilson, *Lectures*, 1790–91).

American Principle Fifteen

Benevolent Provision and Heart of God for Man Is
Recognized by American Founding Fathers

**"And for the support of this *Declaration*, with a firm
reliance on the protection of Divine Providence
we mutually pledge to each other our
Lives, our Fortunes, and our sacred Honor."**
Declaration of Independence

It is the open expression of faith in the nonsectarian God of creation and the unchanging laws of nature that reversed the historic tide of atheistic-secular oppression and deprivation in human history.

"To read the Constitution as the charter for a secular state is to misread history, and to misread it radically. The Constitution was designed to perpetuate a Christian order" (R. J. Rushdoony, *The Nature of the American System,* quoted in "A Christian's View of Civil Government").

"To a generous mind, the public good, as it is the end of government, so it is also such a noble and excellent one, that the prospect of attaining it will animate the pursuit, and being attained, it will reward the pains. The very name of patriotism is indeed become a jest with some men; which would be much stranger than it is, had not so many others made a jest of the thing, serving their own base and wicked ends, under the pretext and color of it. But there will be hypocrites in politics, as well as in religion. Nor ought so sacred a name to fall into contempt, however it may have been prostituted and profaned, to varnish over crimes. And those times are *perilous* indeed, wherein *men shall be* only *lovers of their own selves*, having no concern for the good of the public. Shall we go to the pagans to learn this god-like virtue? Even they can teach it … a reproach not only to his religion, a religion of charity and beneficence, but even to our own common nature, as corrupt and depraved as it is. But how much more infamous were this, in persons of public character, in those on whom the welfare of their country, under providence immediately depends?" (Jonathan Mayhew, D.D. Pastor of the West Church in Boston … to the House of Representatives, 1754, *An Election SERMON*).

Renewed exposure to these *American principles* is our most powerful weapon. It is the light of truth that fortifies the minds of men and women, boys and girls. We believe in them because they reflect the unrelenting power of creation's God. Enslaved for lack of knowledge, Americans need not be.

CHAPTER 2
The Sovereignty of Man under the Impartial God of Creation over Government

In this chapter we can see the rich orthodoxy that brought the universal principles of the *Declaration* to the American mind. That the nation was founded upon the principles of God's Word is well documented by the founding compacts, covenants, and constitutions.

In 1620, the Pilgrims drafted our nation's first self-governing document, the *Mayflower Compact*: "We … having undertaken, for the glory of God, and advancement of the Christian faith, do … solemnly and mutually in ye presence of God, and one another, covenant and combine ourselves together into a civil Body Politic.… And by Virtue hereof to enact, constitute, and frame, such just and equal Laws, Ordinances, Acts, Constitutions and Offices, from time to time, as shall be thought most meet and convenient for the General good of the Colony; unto which we promise all due submission and obedience" (http://www.pilgrimhall.org/compact.htm).

The King of England left the colonists alone for 150 years. Without the albatross of paternalistic authoritarianism, the colonists experienced the benefits of personal responsibility and hard work. People would come together with their pastor or a prominent student of the Bible as moderator and search the scriptures for principles of government that would uphold civility in their community.

In 1630, the famous sermon by John Winthrop, governor of the

Massachusetts Bay Colony, reflected the great sense of purpose that has prevailed since the arrival of the Pilgrims. Later quoted repeatedly by Ronald Reagan, Winthrop declared: "We are to be 'a City upon a hill,' a beacon of light for the world to follow." He continued, "The eyes of all people are upon us. So that if we shall deal falsely with our God in this work we have undertaken, and so cause him to withdraw his present help from us, we shall be made a story and a byword throughout the world."[6]

In 1638, the Fundamental Orders of Connecticut stated: "[We] enter into a combination and confederation together to maintain and preserve the liberty and purity of the gospel of our Lord Jesus Christ which we now profess."[7]

In 1772, Samuel Adams stated: "The right to freedom being a gift from God Almighty ... the rights of Christians may be best understood by reading and carefully studying the institutions of the great Law Giver which are to be found clearly written and promulgated in the New Testament." Disrespect for Authority: Being under authority is not being under control. It is being under God's protection. The help provided by God-ordained authorities can be illustrated by the protective wall or "breakwater" that shields boats in a harbor from devastation. Getting the boat into a harbor may be inconvenient, but the barrier tames the waves and keeps the boats safe. Similarly husbands, parents, employers, and police may be an inconvenience at times, but they play an important role in our progress. God's benevolent instruction is evident at several levels of responsibility and authority for government (Rom. 13:1–3).

The first level of government is individual self-government. Lasting success comes by giving attention to God's standards, the laws of creation's nature that were the norm before man's rebellion opened the door for Satan's influence. Big government, the abundance of police, prisons, and hospitals are the consequences of sinful life practices. When man restrains his own selfish impulses and desires, the tyranny and exploitation of big government can be avoided.

The second level of government is the family. From the beginning, it has been the holy commitment of one man and one woman in marriage that has defeated the will of Satan in his war against civilization. God instituted marriage to facilitate companionship and the nurturing of children in the Truth. The husband cares for his wife in a loving way, and she respects him (Eph. 5:22–33). Parents are responsible for the education of their children. By learning to honor and obey their parents, children also learn to honor the lordship of God and become responsible citizens (Eph. 6:1, 4; Prov. 15:5). The Bible makes it clear that property ownership and wealth come through labor, while laziness produces poverty (Prov. 10:4–5). Recognition of this aspect of the laws of creation's nature benefits families (1 Tim. 5:8; Prov. 31:13–27).

The third level of government is the voluntary union of people belonging to a church. Churches of different denominations to evangelize and edify citizens through Biblical principles for faith and community (1 Tim. 5:17) and discipline (Matt. 18:16–19). Churches also have the Bible mandate to be societal caregivers (1 John 3:17). Families and churches are united in the promotion of citizen self-reliance and limited civil governments.

The fourth level of government is civil government on local, regional, and national levels. Its prime function is to protect the citizens from criminals inside and outside government and from external aggression (Rom. 13:1–4; 1 Pet. 2:13–14).

Following is a listing of the principal lessons to be learned from biblical guidelines about the several levels of government.

1. God instituted civil government.

"For rulers are not a terror to good works, but to the evil. Wilt thou then not be afraid of the power? Do that which is good, and thou shalt have praise of the same: for he is the minister of God to thee for good. But if thou do that which is evil, be afraid; for he beareth not the sword in vain: for he is the minister of God, a revenger to execute wrath upon him that doeth evil" (Rom. 13:3–4).

2. Omnipotent God is sovereign—His authority is over all.

In the history recorded in 1 Samuel 8, the Israelites rejected citizenship responsibilities outlined in scripture and asked to be like other nations and have a king. God gave them a king—an arrangement that was second best to His own authority alone, but better than anarchy.

"But God is the judge: He putteth down one, and setteth up another" (Ps. 75:7). "Now I Nebuchadnezzar praise and extol and honour the King of heaven, all whose works are truth, and His ways judgment: and those that walk in pride He is able to abase" (Dan. 4:37).

3. Government servants are accountable to God.

"For this cause pay ye tribute also: for they are God's ministers, attending continually upon this very thing" (Rom. 13:6).

4. As citizens, we have a moral responsibility to participate and improve civil government.

"Let every soul be subject unto the higher powers. For there is no power but of God: the powers that be are ordained of God. Whosoever therefore resisteth the power, resisteth the ordinance of God: and they that resist shall receive to themselves damnation. For rulers are not a terror to good works, but to the evil. Wilt thou then not be afraid of the power? Do that which is good, and thou shalt have praise of the same: for he is the minister of God to thee for good. But if thou do that which is evil, be afraid; for he beareth not the sword in vain: for he is the minister of God, a revenger to execute wrath upon him that doeth evil" (Rom. 13:1–4).

The Process Toward Independence
from Authoritarian Rule to a New Government

Objections by the original colonies regarding the rule of the British king began when he imposed a series of unjust laws that violated the colonists' rights as British citizens. The colonists objected most vehemently to taxation without representation.

The December 16, 1773, Tea Party: The Colonists were refusing to pay taxes required by the British Parliament because their representatives had not been allowed to participate in tax enforcement decisions. If Americans paid the duty tax on the imported tea they would be acknowledging Parliament's right to tax them. On December 16, 1773, when three shipments of tea were in the Boston harbor the crisis came to a head. The Colonists liked their tea, but in the early evening about 200 descended upon the three ships and dumped the expensive shipments of tea into the harbor waters. This act was monumental and there could no longer be any misunderstanding about the political will of Americans.

In 1774, on September 5, the First Continental Congress came together in Philadelphia with hopes of reaching an agreement with the British king. Alexander Hamilton expressed the colonists' concern in a published pamphlet: "The only distinction between freedom and slavery consists of this: in the former state, man is governed by laws to which he has given his consent, either in person or, by his representative. In the latter he is governed by the will of another."[9]

Alexander Hamilton

In 1775, the Second Continental Congress convened May 10. The goal of the colonies was justice, not independence. On July 5, 1775, the Continental Congress approved the *Olive Branch Petition* and appealed "To the King's Most Excellent Majesty, Most Gracious Sovereign" for reconciliation. The English Parliament responded to this appeal on December 22, 1775, with the *American Prohibitory Act*—a declaration of unrestricted war against the colonists, claiming the right to confiscate their property. Freedom for Americans at that point became a matter of self-defense and necessitated a new republican (republic) government (http://www.manhattanrarebooks-history.com/prohibitory_act.htm).

In 1776, on February 28, George Washington acknowledged a poem written in his honor by Phillis Wheatley. She had been captured in Africa at the age of seven or eight and sold in Boston to John and Susanna Wheatley. They treated her lovingly as a daughter and taught her to read and write; she even learned Latin. An accomplished poet, she was an admirer of the minister George Whitefield and a strong supporter of independence from Great Britain (http://www.lkwdpl.org/wihohio/whea-phi.htm).

The *Declaration of Independence* condemned slavery, but it took a war to make it enforceable. On January 1, 1863, near the end of that war, Abraham Lincoln issued the Emancipation Proclamation that reversed the momentum of slavery (http://www.archives.gov/exhibits/featured_documents/emancipation_proclamation/), (http://www.civilwarhome.com/casualties.htm).

In 1776, on July 4, the Second Continental Congress formally adopted the *Declaration of Independence*, and the American nation was born.

In 1777, on November 15, the *Articles of Confederation*, our nation's first written constitution (which proved to be too weak), was adopted by the Congress. It was not ratified by the states until near the end of the war, but it served as the procedure for governing throughout the war. On March 2, 1781—the day after the *Articles of Confederation* were ratified—the Continental Congress became known as the Confederation of Congress, and the confederacy claimed the title "the United States of America."[10]

From June 1775 to December 1783, upon the recommendation of John Adams, George Washington served as commanding general of the Continental Army. The winter at Valley Forge (1777–78) is an example of the privation suffered by the soldiers who gave their lives for liberty. At this time, George Washington had part of Thomas Paine's *The American Crisis* read to the American army:

> "These are the times that try men's souls. The summer soldier and the sunshine patriot will, in this crisis, shrink from the service of their country; but he that stands by it now, deserves the love and thanks of man and woman. Tyranny, like hell, is not easily conquered; yet we have this consolation with us, that the harder the conflict, the more glorious the triumph. What we obtain too cheap, we esteem too lightly: it is dearness only that gives every thing its value."[11]

From 1775 to 1783, the eight-year War for Independence from authoritarian rule was waged. Its victory was a monumental achievement granted by the providence of God. The signers of the *Declaration of Independence* had pledged their lives, their fortunes, and their sacred honor. Of the fifty-six signers, five were captured by the British as traitors and tortured; twelve had their homes ransacked and burned; two lost their sons serving in the Revolutionary Army; and another had two sons captured. Nine of the fifty-six fought and died from wounds or hardships in the Revolutionary War. In spite of the suffering, not one of the Founding Fathers ever reneged on his commitment to independence (www.snopes.com/history/american/pricepaid.asp).

In 1787, on May 14, a few statesmen began to assemble in Philadelphia to assess the weaknesses of the *Articles of Confederation*. Their meetings soon became a convention for framing a new constitution. On May 25, 1787, George Washington was elected president of the Constitutional Convention. The general outline proposed for the new constitution was presented by Edmund Randolph, governor of Virginia. The outline came from consultation with seven

George Washington

men, among whom James Madison was the most prominent. Their work, spanning almost five months, was an ordeal that required attention to tedious debate, late-hour committee responsibilities, uncomfortable weather, and longing for home. Washington himself, disagreeing with one of the delegates, cautioned that, regardless of whether or not the states would adopt a new constitution, popular fallacies must be avoided: "Let us raise a standard to which the wise and honest can repair; the event is in the hand of God."[12]

When opinions came to an impasse during the Constitutional Convention, Franklin called the delegates to their knees in prayer. The practice of prayer when a United States Senate or House session convenes continues today.[13]

The *Northwest Ordinance* passed earlier by the Continental Congress was very helpful as the new constitution was drafted. It specified the requirements of territories seeking statehood. The ordinance declared: "The fundamental principles of civil and religious liberty, which form the basis whereon these republics, their laws, and constitutions are erected; to fix and establish those principles as the basis of all laws, constitutions, and governments, which forever hereafter shall be formed in the said territory: to provide also for the establishment of States, and permanent government therein, and for their admission to a share in the `federal councils on an equal footing with the original States, at as early periods as may be consistent with the general interest."[14]

Also known as the *Freedom Ordinance,* the *Northwest Ordinance* is a rock-solid example of the nonsectarian religious predicate embraced as constitutional law. When the *Articles of Confederation* was replaced by the new *Constitution*, the *Northwest Ordinance* was passed again and became effective under the new *Constitution*. George Washington signed the *Northwest Ordinance* back into law on August 7, 1789. The *Ordinance* also prohibited slavery in any new state, and Article III specified that **"Religion, morality, and knowledge, being necessary to good government and the happiness of mankind, schools and the means of education, shall forever be encouraged."**[15]

"During this same period of time (July 17 to August 7, 1789), the same men who had implemented the *Northwest Ordinance* were writing the First Amendment to the *Constitution* [prohibiting government officials from interfering with religious freedom, printing press and education competition]."[16]

In 1787, on July 4, consistent with the nationwide custom, Philadelphia celebrated the *Declaration of Independence* with bell ringing, marching with fife and drums, the salute of guns, and speeches. It was Wednesday, and the constitutional delegates had taken the day off. That "The Grand Convention may form a constitution for an eternal Republic!" was the toast of the day. The *Pennsylvania Herald* declared, "With zeal and confidence we expect from the Federal Convention a system of government adequate to the security and preservation of those rights which were promulgated by the ever memorable *Declaration of Independence.*" Because it was conducted in secret, however, the public was unaware that the delegates to the Constitutional Convention were on the verge of failure. Without fair representation, there would be no new constitution. This dilemma was finally solved by allowing all states, big or small, two senators.[17]

In 1787, the Committee of Style and Arrangements, elected by the Constitutional Congress, proceeded to codify what had started out on May 28 as a list of fifteen resolutions presented four months earlier by Edmund Randolph. Twenty-three resolutions for the *Constitution* emerged from their debate. Rearranging them for orderly reading, Governor Morris of Pennsylvania put them together as the *Constitution.* It contained seven articles with short subsections and a preamble that starts with the sovereigns under God, ***"We the People"*** (http://www.history.army.mil/books/revwar/ss/morrisg.htm).

On September 17, 1787, in Philadelphia, members of the Constitutional Convention signed a draft of the *Constitution.* Subject to ratification by nine or more states, America would become a representative republic. The unalienable rights of man as sovereign under God over government are to be guarded by separations of power among the three branches of the central and state governments. Constitutional separations of power also helps to protect against infringement by hierarchical authoritarians or a misled citizen majority (such as occurs in a pure democracy).

Washington, as president of the convention, transmitted the proposed *Constitution* to the people's representatives, who were then still operating under the *Articles of Confederation*. Referring to man's sinful nature and the dangers of collusion of government officials for personal power, Washington wrote: "The great powers to be vested in General Government of the Union and the impropriety of delegating such extensive trust to one body of men is evident: hence results the necessity of a different organization."[18]

**Signing the Constitution, September 17, 1787
with the focus on George Washington.**

The ninth state, New Hampshire, ratified the *Constitution* at its state convention on July 21, 1788. When Congress was informed, it set March 4, 1789, to be the start for the new government. On April 30, 1789, George Washington took the oath of office and became the first president of the United States. Another anxious year passed before that government became fully operational. Fourteen years after the God-honoring *Declaration of Independence* was ratified, the benefits of separation from authoritarian elites became apparent.

By far the most consequential document for government throughout all history is the *Declaration of Independence*. The hitherto inexperienced benefits that enabled America to become the greatest nation on earth rest entirely upon the justification for

displacing the rule of man with rule by impartial, God-honoring law. It provided the philosophical basis for prohibiting actions by government officials that would interfere with citizen sovereignty under God. The people who vote in secret and choose like-minded representatives determine the consensus for government action. Adherence to "self-evident" truths that men are "endowed by their Creator" with "certain unalienable Rights" unleashed citizen creativity and independence from the tyranny and trickery of authoritarians in and out of government.

The purpose of government as a tool for, by, and of the people is spelled out in the preamble forward: "*We the People* of the United States, in Order to form a more perfect Union, establish Justice, insure domestic Tranquility, provide for the common defense, promote the general Welfare, [**meaning common needs that do not conflict with the development of the work ethic and personal self-reliance**] and secure the Blessings of Liberty to ourselves and our Posterity, do ordain and establish this Constitution for the United States of America."

One historian points out that the preamble contains seven action words: form, establish, insure, provide, promote, secure, and ordain. The *Constitution* concludes: "Done in convention by the unanimous consent of the States present on the seventeenth day of September in the year of our Lord one thousand seven hundred and eighty-seven and of the **independence [*Declaration of Independence,* founded upon the sovereignty of the benevolent God of creation and of the Bible]** of the United States of America the twelfth [**adopted twelve years earlier**]. In witness whereof we have hereunto subscribed our names."[19]

In 1791, on July 19, having come through several months of severe personal depression because of continuing chaos in the states, George Washington wrote in a letter to Catherine Macaulay Graham: "The United States enjoys a scene of prosperity and tranquility under the new government, that could hardly have been hoped for."[20]

In 1792, on March 11, Washington explained: "I am sure there never was a people who had more reason to acknowledge a Divine interposition in their affairs than those of the United States; and I should be pained to believe that they have forgotten that Agency which was so often manifested during our revolution, or that they failed to consider the omnipotence of that God who is alone able to protect them."[21]

Charles Pinckney

Charles Pickering, who at the outset of the convention doubted the success of the undertaking, was amazed at the final result: "Nothing less than that superintending hand of Providence, that so miraculously carried us through the war, could have brought it [the *Constitution*] about so complete, upon the whole."[22]

A century later, William Gladstone, one of Britain's greatest prime ministers, proclaimed the American *Constitution* to be "the most wonderful work ever struck off by the brain and purpose of man."[23]

The *Constitution of the United States* has survived many times longer than any other constitution. For example, in the last two hundred years, France has gone through seven different government charters, and Italy forty. "In God Is Our Trust," emblazoned in "The Star-Spangled Banner" (official national anthem of the United States), takes elitists of every stripe out of the authority equation.

CHAPTER 3
Man May Prosper in Freedom If He Chooses to Honor the Will of Creation's God

The benefits of the Bible to society and governments were recognized by the Founding Fathers. The Bible was "recommended to American citizens by the Confederation Congress on September 12, 1782" (*Religion and the Founding of the American Republic*, James H. Hutson, Washington, DC: Library of Congress, 1998, Preface and pp. 57–58).

God's standard for truth is the most fundamental moral category in the universe. Truth separates traditional American values (theistic belief) from the old European secular philosophy (atheistic belief about life's origin, meaning, and purpose). Abel, who had chosen to follow the God of absolute truth, was slain by Cain, who, abiding by the impulses of the flesh, had chosen to follow his own version of truth. It is this same war of divergent cultures that is now raging between the "In God We Trust" of Americans and the cultish atheism of old European secular philosophy.

During the controversy over the French Revolution (which provided the pattern for communism), Edmund Burke wrote this about moral and political truth: "We know that we have made no discoveries; and we think that no discoveries remain to be made in morality; nor many in the great principles of government, nor in the idea of liberty, which were understood long before we were born, altogether as well as they will be after the grave has heaped its mould upon our presumption, and the silent tomb shall have imposed its law on our pert loquacity." In response to the question, "What is liberty?" he stated: "Mere liberty without other forces working in the sphere that it opens up is only another name for license" (Edmund Burke's *Reflections on the Revolution in France*, 1790, London: Henry G. Bohn, 1864 extract, 129).

The sovereignty of constitutional government is clearly made subordinate to the sovereignty of certain God-given rights of the citizens who ratified it. This distinguishes the meaning of liberty of individuals in America. They can exercise their independence and capacity to make better and differing decisions. This contrasts from the demands of secular academician with communistic, socialistic, and liberal leanings, who reject the citizen's capacity for self-rule and expect conformity to cultish political correctness based upon incalculable and changeable decrees (see Chapter 5).

The *Bill of Rights* law is spiritual in the sense that it upholds the unalienable right of the people to follow God's prescription for happiness without fear of authoritarian reprisals. The idea is economic as well, because people, having the right to life, also have the right to work and to use the fruits of their labor to sustain life.

The God of creation is identified by the Bible as the "Good Shepherd." It is this same God who gave the Ten Commandments to mankind through Moses. The good Shepherd does not dictate and control. When a lamb falls and breaks its leg, the shepherd will place a splint on the leg and carry the lamb until it heals. Then, hoping the lamb has learned a lesson, it is able to run again. God admonishes, but unlike those allied with Satan, He will not deceive and seek to by-pass a person's common sense to force worldly compliance (atheistic political correctness). When a person chooses to run his life according to God's Word, he has chosen to be under the "Shepherd's" protection.

The laws of creation's nature include the perimeters for civil behavior provided by the Ten Commandments (Exod. 20 and Deut. 5). Because of the universal benefits that come from applying the Commandments, they are a common part of the moral religions throughout the world. Prior to the time that supremacist judges embraced the intolerance of a tiny minority (the laws of man), the rest of us had the benefits that come when the Commandments were emphasized in the schools and on public properties throughout the nation.

Sculpture in the Supreme Court

Americans recognize that the promotion of life-building attitudes is important, but that it is not right to punish harmful attitudes that have not been expressed by criminal actions. *"We, The People"* place the consequences of attitudes, good or bad, in the hand of God, Who sees and hears all. Over time, the failure to police one's own thoughts renders severe punishments in direct proportion to the evil being entertained. These six commandments pertain directly to such matters of the heart:

Honor your father and mother.

You shall have no other gods before Me.

You shall not take the name of the LORD your God in vain.

Remember the Sabbath day, to keep it holy.

You shall not make for yourself a graven image.

You shall not covet your neighbor's house; you shall not covet your neighbor's wife, nor his male servant, nor his female servant, nor his ox, nor his donkey, nor anything that is your neighbor's.

Four of the commandments provide the foundation for civil and criminal law in America:

You shall not murder (the right to life).

You shall not commit adultery (the sanctity of marriage).

You shall not steal (the right to own property).
You shall not bear false witness against your neighbor (the right to be truthfully represented).

It is citizen support for moral absolutes reflected in the Ten Commandments that promotes the passage of good laws by elected representatives. Only this type of government can prevail over the curse of moral relativism practiced by the masters of political deception.

> To justify taxpayer support, educators must teach the truth about the God-honoring *Declaration of Independence* and Ten Commandments that have enabled Americans to change a wilderness into the greatest nation on earth.

Secular authoritarians insist upon what they call a "living constitution" that has an open-minded disconnect from moral absolutes. As has been attributed to Dostoevsky among others, "If God is dead, then anything is permitted." The colossal failure of secularized education flowing from teachers unions and tenure privileges, which subordinates citizen sovereignty, is the damning consequence of atheistic-secular politics. The *Constitution* becomes a mere political document for manipulation by authoritarians who show themselves to be enemies of family, human dignity, and limited government.

Regardless of the arguments advanced by those who reject the intent of the *Constitution*, the Rule of Law means that the government is limited in all of its actions by the rules fixed and ratified beforehand. This is the context within which legislation, court decisions, and administrative directives at all levels of government must fit.

For those who deny the important role of morality, here is its meaning from Merriam-Webster: **1 a:** of or relating to principles of right and wrong in behavior: ETHICAL <moral judgments>; **b:** expressing or teaching a conception of right behavior <a moral poem>; **c:** conforming to a standard of right behavior; **d:** sanctioned by or operative on one's conscience or ethical judgment <a moral obligation>; **e :** capable of right and wrong action <a moral agent>.

Americans determined to protect liberty reject the "living constitution" because it leaves society vulnerable to political deception. Constitutional government by "written and permanent law" requires an amendment that is acceptable to the people before a change in its provisions is acceptable. Faithfulness to this process protects society from political deception and the convolution associated with government by incalculable and changeable decrees (see Chapter 5).

Those who reject the rule of law based upon moral absolutes are like ships without an anchor.

The Illusion Of Reality
(Rebellion against God / incalculable and changeable decrees)

Ship Without an Anchor—Education and Laws
Waxing Worse and Worse

In Denial of Truth—
The Godless Relativistic Presupposition

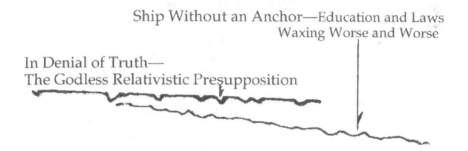

This drift is illustrated by decisions made by judges who set precedents that ignore and that override the meaning of the *Constitution*. An example of the foolishness of the rule of man rather than the rule of law is the US Court of Appeals for the Ninth Circuit's ruling on November 2, 2005, that parents' fundamental right to control the upbringing of their children "does not extend beyond the threshold of the school door," and that a government school has the right to provide its students with "whatever information it wishes to provide, sexual or otherwise" (*Fields v. School District*, No. 03-56499, D.C. No. CV-03-00457-JVS). This unconscionable judge-made law further strengthens the arms of union bosses, leftist teachers, and radicals, if any, on school boards.

THE WAR AGAINST GOD

The old European secular philosophy,***** as defined in this book, includes secular humanists and other atheistic sects, such as the followers of Friedrich Nietzsche, Karl Marx, Charles Darwin, Professor John Dewey, and Fabian socialist John Maynard Keynes. Their agenda is obvious. It is the elimination of God and the moral predicate for law. Their belief is expressed in the *Humanist Manifesto*: "No deity will save us; we must save ourselves." The first *Humanist Manifesto*, written in 1933, was published with thirty-four signatories including the educator John Dewey (Paul Kurtz, tenured radical professor, State University of New York at Buffalo, *Humanist Manifesto II*, 2).

"The attempt by the rulers of a nation [France] to destroy all religious opinion, and to pervert a whole nation to atheism ... [and] to establish atheism on the ruins of Christianity [is] to deprive mankind of its best consolations and most animating hopes, and to make a gloomy desert of the universe" (James D. Richardson, citing Alexander Hamilton

---

***** The old European secular philosophy is a reflection of the hope in a fantasy world. Marxists used socialist slogans, such as "From each according to his ability, to each according to his needs." The Soviet Socialist Union lasted but a whiff in time in spite of their great universities, KGB (secret police), a worldwide propaganda machine, and military aggression (1917–91). Liberals in present-day America justify socialism by saying that we are a wealthy nation. Some people in America who budget wisely and have a good income do have wealth, but the truth is that the American government is broke. The Soviets not only funded their government by an excessive tax on the Russian people, but they also extracted a tax from over a dozen captive countries—and they still went broke. Liberal politicians create a supportive voting block by promising them wealth redistribution. This comes by stealing from Americans (excessive tax), stealing from future generations (debt obligation), and the added tax of interest on the debt. When government officials are allowed to continue imposing high taxes, the incentive of the people to work hard and save is greatly diminished and the base for taxation is gradually destroyed. Also, the ability of the people to support churches and missionaries and to assist the poor is greatly diminished. At the time of this writing, the national debt is over 14 trillion dollars. The revenue left after funding excessive government is not enough to pay the interest, so the shortage must be added to the principal indebtedness.

from October 3, 1789, in *A Compilation of the Messages and Papers of the Presidents, 1789–1897*, published by Congress, 1899, Vol. I, 64).

Without exception, rejection of creation's God and freedom for religious competition over the broad spectrum of private and public life gives rise to moral revisionism.

Since the Supreme Court decision *Everson v. Board of Education* in 1947, tenured radical teachers have sought to taken God out of education and ultimately turned the tide of education against the family. Karl Marx attacked the family. He appealed to academia and others for the "abolition of the family." "The bourgeois clap-trap about the family and education, about the hallowed correlation of parent and child" is "disgusting" (Karl Marx and Frederick Engels, *Manifesto of the Communist Party, 1848,* http://www.anu.edu.au/polsci/ marx/classics/ manifesto.html).

Judith Stacey, a highly regarded member of the public school primary and secondary education faculty at the University of California (Davis campus), declared: "The 'family' is not here to stay. All democratic people, whatever their kinship preferences, should work to hasten its demise" ("Rights and Rites," *The Washington Times*, March 29, 1993).

Dr. John Dewey, a proponent of teacher employment guarantees at taxpayer expense, is the acknowledged father of modern-day public education. He was an admirer of Margaret Sanger, Humanist of the Year in 1967 and a founder of Planned Parenthood. Sanger also founded the publication *The Woman Rebel,* whose slogan was "No Gods! No Masters!" Her first edition denounced marriage as a "degenerate institution" and sexual modesty as "obscene prudery" (George Grant, *Legacy of Planned Parenthood,* Wolgemuth & Hyatt, Publishers, Inc).

Dr. John Dewey presents Margaret Sanger with the
American Women's Association Medal, 1932.

The religious presupposition for the secular humanist mind-set comes from Charles Darwin's book *Origin of the Species*. Those who adopted Darwin's God-rejecting assumption about the origin, meaning, and purpose of life have *no* dependable standards upon which to establish human equality, morality, or representative government. Truth for them is what man himself chooses at any given time and circumstance. Standards are based on wishes, perceptions, and mortal goals, rather than on established knowledge, objective facts, or principles.

"These [atheist] teachers must embody the same selfless dedication as the most rabid fundamentalist preachers, for they will be ministers of another sort, utilizing a classroom instead of a pulpit to convey humanist [atheistic] values in whatever subject they teach, regardless of the education level—preschool, daycare or large state university. The classroom must and will become an area of conflict between the old and the new—the rotting corpse of Christianity" (*The Humanist*, January/February 1983).

Monopoly unions are used by the champions of old European philosophy to consolidate political power. When legislators succumbed to handouts from leftist National Education Association unions, laws began to turn against traditional American law and citizen self-government. The nonpartisan *Iowa Family Policy Center News Letter*, March 2008, reports that "Iowa Democrats have accepted $440,000 from out-of-state homosexual activists, with $170,000 going directly to Democrat legislators facing hotly contested races [Iowa Ethics and Campaign Disclosure]." Involving at least $40 million nationwide in 2008, the financial and political influence of NEA leftists is immense (*Education Reporter, # 272*, Eagle Forum, St. Louis, MO). Backed up by the 1947 Supreme Court decision *Everson v. Board of Education,* militant objectors to the American principles and creed bullied their way into controlling the atmosphere of American public schools.

George Weigel, highly respected author, said at a Seattle Pacific University Symposium of this move away from representative citizen control over government policies: "It not only seemed to me an act of infidelity toward the past, it seemed to imply a program for the future, namely, state-enforced secularism." In an interview with Kathleen Braden, Weigel laments political decisions made bureaucratically rather than democratically, according to the popular will, and trumpets the need for spiritual revival in America and for citizen action as "salt and light" (George Weigel, author of *The Cube and the Cathedral,* "A Conversation With George Weigel," *Response* Magazine, Seattle Pacific University, Seattle, Washington, Autumn 2007, 18–20).

A report by the nonpartisan Commission on Excellence in Education remains the premier American study of problems in public education. It states: "The educational foundations of our society are presently being eroded by a rising tide of mediocrity that threatens our very future as a Nation and a people ... If an unfriendly foreign power had attempted to impose on America the educational performance that exists today, we might well have viewed it as an act of war." The report laments "the deconstruct of the moral and spiritual strengths which knit together the very fabric of our society" (*A Nation at Risk*, the National Commission on Excellence in Education, April 26, 1983, http://www.ed.gov/pubs/NatAtRisk/risk.html).

Scholastic Aptitude Test (SAT) scores have declined, and today the United States ranks academically near the bottom of the world's industrialized nations. College seniors have no better grasp of general cultural knowledge than did high school graduates in the 1950s. The average correct responses for modern college seniors on a series of questions was 53.5 percent, compared to 54.5 percent of high school graduates in 1955 (survey by Zogby International, April 2002, for the Princeton, New Jersey-based National Association of Scholars, presented by NAS President Stephen H. Balch in December 2002).

In the fall of 2005, researchers at the University of Connecticut's National Civic Literacy Board conducted a survey of some 14,000 freshmen and seniors at fifty colleges and universities. Students were asked sixty multiple-choice questions to measure their knowledge in four subject areas: America's history, government, international relations, and market economy. Seniors, on average, failed all four subjects, and their overall average score was 53.2 percent. (*The Coming Crisis in Citizenship: Higher Education's Failure to Teach America's History and Institutions*, 09/26/2006, Intercollegiate Studies Institute's National Civic Board Report. See http://content.usatoday.com/community/tags/topic.aspx?r eq=tag&tag=Intercollegiate+Studies+Institute).

Supremacist judges, liberals (progressive) in education, and their converts in the media have deceived millions of people into believing that privacy rights, social justice, and diversity require public acceptance of evil life practices, homosexuality, and baby genocide. The loss of American values arises directly from unelected liberal judges-turned-legislators and the ensuing defilement of traditional American jurisprudence.

"Truth [when communicated] is great and will prevail if left to herself ... she is the proper and sufficient antagonist to error, and has nothing to fear from the conflict, unless by human interposition disarmed of her natural weapons, free argument and debate, errors ceasing to be dangerous when it is permitted freely to contradict them" *(Virginia Statute of Religious Liberty*, 1786, cited by Hamilton Abert

Long, *The American Ideal of 1776*, Philadelphia: Heritage Books Inc., 1963, xxii).

"America has freed more human beings from the clutches of evil than any [other] nation on earth, and we are only a relatively young country. Even though continental Europe, in its posture of pseudo-sophistication, might consider us the country cousin of the family of nations, when these same Europeans needed to be rescued—often from themselves—we were there to rescue them. We have done it many times and in many ways, around the world. At enormous costs to ourselves, we have gone into (and out of) dozens of nations in order to make the world a better place—even those nations that were our deadliest enemies, like Germany and Japan after World War II. What MacArthur did in Japan, and what the Marshall Plan accomplished in Europe, are without historical equal, and they indicate what we think our high calling on the planet really is! They also indicate the American penchant for forgiveness and generosity, which surpasses all others" (Dr. Jack Wheeler, *The Ugly Liberal American,* page 4, quoted by *The Schwarz Report*, May 2008, Volume 48, number 5).

CHAPTER 4
America's Civic Religion and the Deeper Personal Faith of Our Nation's Founders

In 1952, Justice William O. Douglas wrote, "We are a religious people and our institutions presuppose a Supreme Being."[24]

There are two classifications for religion in America: civic religion and the personal faith of individuals—their manner of worship, fellowship, and practice.

The first of these two classifications for religion in America is civic religion. A primary duty of government officials and most certainly the duty of professors and teachers whose salaries are funded by taxpayers is to promote the liberating principles of the nonsectarian American civic creed (see Chapters 1 and 2).

The *Declaration of Independence* (July 1776), the *Articles of Confederation* (drafted 1777, ratified 1781), and the *Constitution* (ratified 1788) have been classified as the most important American charters. Collectively they received a total of 143 signatures from 118 people. By their affirmations, these individuals represented themselves to be believers in the providence of God, and they did so at the risk of being hung by British soldiers.

Professor Donald S. Lutz of the University of Houston describes a ten-year study during which he and others assembled the writings and deliberations of the American Founding Fathers.[25] The study brought into focus important sources that were used when determining priorities for the American *Constitution*. Aside from quotations from the Bible, the sources relied upon most by the Founding Fathers were the writings of Montesquieu, Blackstone, and Locke.

Montesquieu's best-known work was *The Spirit of Laws*. He emphasized the importance of separating the personnel and duties for the legislative, executive, and judicial branches of government. The purpose of this separation of power was to prevent abuse of the people's rights as sovereigns over government (Isa. 33:22 and Jer. 17). Blackstone emphasized the Law of Nature (man's nature both before and after the fall) and Revealed Law (scripture). His *Commentaries on the Common Law of England* was especially practical for the new nation. Locke, born into a Puritan family and son of a lawyer, provided the "Essay Concerning Human Understanding" and two treatises "On Civil Government." His "life, liberty, or property" phrase is part of both the Fifth and Fourteenth Amendments to the *Constitution*.

The chief source for the Founding Fathers' understanding was the Bible. It was cited three times more often than were these three men combined. Thirty-four percent of all ideas referred to by the constitutional delegates came directly from the Old and New Testament books. Furthermore, 60 percent of the references to opinions of Montesquieu, Blackstone, and Locke. were drawn from the Bible. The most frequently quoted book was the Old Testament book of Deuteronomy.

The following are quotes cited in the introduction to *Halley's Bible Handbook* authored by Henry H. Halley and published by Zondervan, Grand Rapids, MI (republished since 1924):

Abraham Lincoln: "I believe the Bible is the best gift God has ever given to man."
W. E. Gladstone: "The Bible is stamped with a Specialty of Origin, and an immeasurable distance separates it from all competitors."
Thomas Huxley: "The Bible has been the Magna Carta of the poor and oppressed. The human race is not in a position to dispense with it."
Sir Isaac Newton: "There are more sure marks of authenticity in the Bible than in any profane history."

George Washington: "It is impossible to rightly govern the world without God and the Bible."

George Washington served as a delegate to the Continental Congress and as commander in chief of the Continental Army. He later presided over the Constitutional Convention and finally served as the first president of the United States. He praised the effectiveness of critics for insisting upon the first ten amendments to the *United States Constitution,* and he complemented both James Madison and Alexander Hamilton for their work in writing the *Federalist Papers*, saying, they "have thrown new light upon the science of government; they have given the rights of man a full and fair discussion, and explained them in so clear and forcible a manner as cannot fail to make a lasting impression" (http://teachingamericanhistory.org/library/index.asp?document=378).

During the swearing-in ceremony for the first president of the United States, George Washington placed his hand over Genesis, Chapter 49 in the Holy Bible. Of his own volition, he took the oath of office concluding with the precedent setting predicate, "So help me God." Immediately the new president bent down and kissed the sacred book (Peter A. Lillback with Jerry Newcombe, *George Washington's Sacred Fire*, Bryn Mawr, Pennsylvania, Dickson Press, 2006, p. 224)

In his Farewell Address, Washington reminded Americans that: "Of all the dispositions and habits which lead to political prosperity, religion and morality are indispensable supports. In vain would that man claim the tribute of patriotism, who should labor to subvert these great pillars of human happiness, these firmest props of the duties of men and citizens. The mere politician, equally with the pious man, ought to respect and to cherish them. A volume could not trace all their connections with private and public felicity. Let it simply be asked: Where is the security for property, for reputation, for life, if the sense of religious obligation deserts the oaths which are the instruments of investigation in courts of justice? And let us with caution indulge the supposition that morality can be maintained without religion. Whatever may be conceded to the influence of refined education on minds of peculiar structure, reason and experience both forbid us to expect that national morality can prevail in exclusion of religious principle."[26]

Presidents, as well as many other citizens, attended church services held on Sundays in the United States Capitol building. President Thomas Jefferson, "during his whole administration, 1801–1809, was a most regular church attendant," documents James H. Hutson in *Religion and the Founding of the American Republic*. Ministers of several Christian denominations conducted the services. Honoring the nonsectarian God

Thomas Jefferson

of creation in public and on government property is an important manifestation of civic faith. In addition to attending church services in the Capitol building, Thomas Jefferson made significant financial contributions to that ministry.

"After the Civil War, from 1865–1868, the House of Representatives in Washington, D.C., permitted the newly organized First Congregational Church of Washington to use its chambers for church and Sunday school services. During that same time, specifically on May 13, 1866, Congress passed the Fourteenth Amendment which, according to some later judicial foolishness, forbids religious activities on public property."[27]

Editors of the book *Speeches That Changed the World* started with the Ten Commandments (Exod. 20: 1–17) and Christ's Sermon on the Mount (Matt. 5–7). These editors recognized the good that believers have contributed to society and the superior quality of the Bible as literature. Later in *Speeches That Changed the World* are speeches by two Darwinian evolutionists, Adolf Hitler and Joseph Stalin. Their leadership did influence the world. The murder of millions of innocent people demonstrates the depths to which the open-mindedness of Darwin's *Origin of the Species* dogma can take man.[28]

Addressing Congress, Benjamin Rush, signer of the *Declaration of Independence,* proclaimed: "I anticipate nothing but suffering to the human race while the present systems of paganism, deism, and atheism prevail in the world."[29]

On September 25, 1789, Congress requested unanimously that President Washington proclaim a national day of thanksgiving and prayer. This is the same Congress that on the same day approved the final draft of the First Amendment to protect the people's rights to religious freedom from suppression by government administrators, judges, or legislators. President Washington proclaimed on October 3, 1798: "Whereas it is the duty of all nations to acknowledge the providence of Almighty God, to obey His will, to be grateful for His benefits, and humbly to implore His protection and favor ... Now, therefore, I do recommend ... that we may then all unite in rendering unto Him our sincere and humble thanks for His kind care and protection of the people of this country previous to their becoming a nation; for the signal and manifold mercies and the favorable interpositions of His providence in the course and conclusion of the late war; for the great degree of tranquility, union, and plenty which we have since enjoyed; for the peaceable and rational manner in which we have been enabled to establish constitutions of government for our safety and happiness, and particularly the national one now lately instituted; for the civil and religious liberty with which we are blessed ... And also that we may then unite in most humbly offering our prayers and supplications to the great Lord and Ruler of Nations, and beseech Him to pardon our national and other transgressions ... to promote the knowledge and practice of true religion and virtue."[30]

Contemporary liberals insist that the *Declaration of Independence* has no relevance to the *Constitution of the United States*. Nothing could be further from the truth. That was the argument used by Stephen A. Douglas in the historic Lincoln-Douglas debates. Douglas, who practiced constitutional revisionism, rejected Abraham Lincoln's insistence that moral judgment applies to situations calling for decision. Lincoln quoted from the *Declaration of Independence* to affirm the moral predicate of constitutional law.

The following is from Lincoln's Peoria speech, October 16, 1854: "I have quoted so much [of the *Declaration*] at this time to show that according to our ancient faith, the just powers of government are derived from the consent of the governed. Now the relation of masters and slaves is, *pro tanto*, a total violation of this principle. The master not only governs the slave without his consent: but he governs him by a set of rules altogether different from those he prescribes for himself. Allow all the governed an equal voice in their government, and that, and that only, is self-government." Harry V. Jaffa, reviewing Lincoln's speech, added, "Aristotle, in his only reference to piety in the *Nicomachean Ethics*, says that virtue requires us to honor truth before our friends. That is because we would not otherwise be worth having as friends."[31]

Governments and authoritarians are not the source of man's rights. Government is but a tool that should be used to protect man's right to worship the creation's God. This impartial Creator of life ordained and established the unalienable human rights outlined in the *Declaration of Independence* that cause representative governments to follow the rule of established law, not the arbitrary rule of man. Legislators, administrators, and judges who use laws (the power of government) to establish religious, ideological, or employee union monopolies are fascistic. Fascism is a word used to identify the enemies of representative governments and governments limited for the protection of the people's freedom to be informed and to choose.

American courts and judges honored the benevolent providence of God unabashedly. "On Monday last the Circuit Court [Portsmouth, NH, May 24, 1800] of the United States was opened in this town.

The Hon. Judge Paterson presided. After the Jury was impaneled, the Judge delivered a most elegant and appropriate charge ... Religion and morality were pleasingly inculcated and enforced as being necessary to good government, good order, and good laws, for 'when the righteous are in authority, the people rejoice [Proverbs 29:2]' ... After the charge was delivered, the Rev. Mr. [Timothy] Alden addressed the Throne of Grace in an excellent, well adapted prayer."[32]

In 1892, the Supreme Court of the United States cited eighty-seven precedents and proclaimed: "Our laws and our institutions must necessarily be based upon and embody the teachings of the Redeemer of Mankind. It is impossible that it should be otherwise: and in this sense and to the extent our civilization and our institutions are emphatically Christian ... This is a religious people. This is historically true. From the discovery of this continent to the present hour, there is a single voice making this affirmation ... we find everywhere a clear recognition of the same truth."[33]

The Supreme Court was saying that they had reviewed eighty-seven decisions for settling disputes by previous courts, and they all followed Biblical principles of right and wrong. Respect for this truth can be traced historically to the founders' Christian faith. Human authoritarianism was rejected. The principles of the nonsectarian God of creation, spoken of in the American *Declaration of Independence* and the *Bill of Rights* were viewed as supreme.

Dwight Eisenhower

Legislation drafted by the United States Senate and House of Representatives adding the words "under God" to the American Pledge of Allegiance was signed by President Eisenhower in 1954. In 1964, the Supreme Court rejected a challenge to the law.

In 1954, Congress ordered that "a room with facilities for prayer and meditation ..." be made available in the United States Capitol. The seventh edition of *The Capitol*, an official publication of the United States Congress, describes the stained-glass window of the Congressional Prayer Room:

"The history that gives this room its inspirational lift is centered in the stained glass window. George Washington kneeling in prayer … is the focus of the composition … Behind Washington a prayer is etched: 'Preserve me, O God, for in Thee I put my trust," the first verse of the sixteenth Psalm. There are upper and lower medallions representing the two sides of the Great Seal of the United States. On these are inscribed the phrases: *annuit coeptis*—'God has favored our undertakings'—and *novus ordo seclorum*—'A new order of the ages is born.' Under the upper medallion is the phrase from Lincoln's immortal Gettysburg Address, 'This Nation under God.'… The two lower corners of the window each show the Holy Scriptures, an open book and a candle, signifying the light from God's law, 'Thy Word is a lamp unto my feet and a light unto my path' [Psalm 119:105]."

The obligations that apply to theistic religions also apply to atheistic religions! By refusing to admit that faith-dependent atheism is religious (concerned with beliefs about origin, meaning, and purpose of life), secular militants hope to escape responsibility for civil standards of morality. While demanding supremacy for their God-rejecting faith, they deny public freedom for the Creator-based civic creed in the soft sciences, most particularly in the study of biology, economics, American government, history, and judicial foundations. When secular militants succeed here, they then move to deny belief in God period, even as the basis for personal faith.

Student understanding of American civic religion in taxpayer-funded schools is a foremost curriculum requirement. By excluding the denominational creeds and biases that tend to be divisive, the people unify in support of governments that honor "In God We Trust" as a nonsectarian creed.

The second of the two classifications of religion in America is the personal faith of individuals—their manner of worship, fellowship, and practice. The Founding Fathers were not only avid Creationists; they were members of many different church denominations, and the vast majority of them were in their personal faith, born-again Christians.[34]

"Therefore if any man be in Christ, he is a new creature: old things are passed away; behold, all things are become new" (2 Cor. 5:17).

For you have been "born again, not of corruptible seed, but of incorruptible, by the word of God, which liveth and abideth for ever" (1 Pet. 1:23).

Personal faith is primary, and the nonsectarian American civic religion which so vital to public education is the composite result. The purity of America's civic religion that advances individual liberty is totally dependent on religious freedom, which in turn requires freedom from intimidation by government-established ideologues (educators, clergy, and so on).

Public school students must be taught to understand and appreciate the importance of the all-encompassing concept of an impartial, nonsectarian God and creation's nature, American civic religion. Inculcation, however, in the personal faith relating to worship and a denomination's religious doctrine must not be allowed to become a function of government education.

The Founding Fathers who adopted the *Declaration of Independence* and the *Constitution* came from eleven Christian groups that held different views about church ordinances, baptism, communion, church polity, discipline, worship, and so on (http://www.adherents.com/gov/Founding_Fathers_Religion.html).

Alexander Hamilton said in an essay published soon after the framing convention adjourned: "For my own part, I sincerely esteem it a system, which, without the finger of God, never could have been suggested and agreed upon by such a diversity of interests" (http://www.zeios.com/OurRepublic/Author/22).
Madison expressed this same belief in *The Federalist* No. 37.

"Hast thou not known? hast thou not heard, [that] the everlasting God, the LORD, the Creator of the ends of the earth, fainteth not, neither is weary? [there is] no searching of his understanding. He giveth power to the faint; and to [them that have] no might he increaseth strength. Even the youths shall faint and be weary, and the young men shall utterly fall: But they that wait upon the LORD shall renew [their] strength; they shall mount up with wings as eagles; they shall run, and not be weary; [and] they shall walk, and not faint" (Isa. 10:28–31).

In the Judeo-Christian Bible, we learn of the personal faith shared by many different Christian denominations: "For God so loved the world, that He gave His only begotten Son, that whosoever believeth in Him should not perish, but have everlasting life. For God sent not His Son into the world to condemn the world; but that the world through Him might be saved" (John 3:16–17).

Justice and grace meet at the cross of Calvary, where the price of sin was paid by Christ, Who loves us more than we love ourselves. The following passages provide some context for the phrase "born again": John 3:16–17 and Romans 5:8–9, 10:9–13. When individuals acknowledge their need for forgiveness and humbly accept God's gift of salvation from the penalty of sin, a divine God-to-man cooperative becomes a reality.

Colonial churches were clearly Biblical. Schools such as Harvard and the local public grade schools were Bible-based and evangelical. Noah Webster (1758–1843), a contributor to the *Constitution* and widely acknowledged as the most influential educator for over a hundred years, unabashedly proclaimed his conversion to Christ during a campus revival at Yale (http://yalestandard. com/chaunceygoodrich.aspx).

Noah Webster

Webster, who was skilled in six languages, published the *American Dictionary of the English Language* in 1828. In 1833, he said: "It is extremely important to our nation, in a political as well as religious view, that all possible authority and influence should be given to the scriptures, for these furnish the best principles of civil liberty and the most effectual support of republican (meaning republic) government."

The two classifications of religion, civic and personal, can live openly side by side. The fact that Americans are free to share their personal religious convictions in public is vital, even though it may be controversial, because the different beliefs can then be known, evaluated and may be chosen. This is to be respected.

CHAPTER 5
Government by Written and Permanent Law

"Government is frequently and aptly classed under two descriptions, a government of FORCE [arbitrary and changeable decrees imposed by authoritarians], and a government of LAWS [governments that derive 'their just powers from the consent of the governed];' the first is the definition of despotism—the last Liberty" (Alexander Hamilton, *Tully Papers* 1794).[35]

The move away from totalitarian governments to the American Republic and freedom resulted with changes in authority. Kings, popes, academician elites, and others claimed to be supreme. This is comparable to what self-indulgent judges are now doing in America. Rejecting the meaning and intent of the Constitution, they seek to impose societal values of their own choosing. When federal laws dealing with local concerns descend downward, they become oppressive and often harmful to society. A significant advance away from totalitarian law occurred when English Barons rebelled against King John and forced him to sign the Magna Carta on June 15, 1215. In the United States, people looked to creation's God for higher authority. No longer captive to big government, religious liberty and free speech, intended by First Amendment law, thrived. Corruption is limited when the development of law comes from the people unless, of course, they become estranged from God and the moral certainties of creation's nature. When this happens the people become vulnerable to exploitation and paternalistic authoritarians.

George Washington in his Farewell Address reminded future generations that they cannot neglect the personal responsibility for upholding the moral predicate for law: "It is easy to foresee, that from different causes and from different quarters, much pains will be taken, many artifices employed, to weaken in your minds the conviction of this truth ('keep alive the spirit of Liberty'); as this is the point in your political fortress against which the batteries of internal and external enemies will be most constantly and actively directed."[36]

What sets the American *Constitution* apart from those of so many other nations is that its use is rooted in the Higher Authority Judeo-Christian tradition for civil order. The *Constitution* is a tool composed of directives, checks, and obstacles. When the principles of the Creator-based *Declaration* articulated in the *Bill of Rights* are upheld, the obstacles built into the *Constitution* become morally effective, and it becomes difficult for government employees to empower a partisan political agenda or line their pockets with taxpayers' money.

The American system of government is a Federal Republic, meaning a confederation of many—a central government and state governments. James Madison describes the American system as "a Republic—a federation, or combination, of central and state republics—under which: the different governments will control each other.…" (*Federalist* No. 51).

The federal and state governments are Republics which are distinguished by the fact that they are **representative** and limited in their power by **written Constitutions** (*Federalist* No. 45). The citizen electorate adopts the Constitutions, and they are only changeable from the original through amendment by the people. The powers are divided between the legislative, executive and judicial branches of government which remain subject to the sovereignty of the people (electorate) under creation's God per the *Declaration of Independence*. "The United States shall guarantee to every State in this Union a Republican Form of Government, and shall protect each of them against Invasion; and on Application of the Legislature, or of the Executive (when the Legislature cannot be convened) against domestic Violence," Article IV, Section 4 of the Federal government *Constitution*.

Washington wrote: "Government is not reason; it is not eloquent; it is force. Like fire, it is a dangerous servant and a fearful master."[37]

The principles we have listed in Chapter 1 are changeless, practical, and appropriate for government "by written and permanent law." "All men ... are endowed by their Creator with certain unalienable Rights, that among these are Life, Liberty and the pursuit of Happiness." "In questions of power [Thomas Jefferson wrote] let no more be heard of confidence in man, but bind him down from mischief by the chains of the *Constitution*."[38]

In the words of Chief Justice John Roberts: "Governments in world history have so often abused the power, and people have suffered because of it. The framers decided they were going to lay down some rules to try to keep that from happening—that's what the *Constitution* is. Of all the major written constitutions in history it's the shortest. It's not an elaborate code. They were laying down basic principles that they wanted to endure and it is timeless.... our *Constitution* is different from a lot of others. Many countries that have constitutions—they're really just political documents."[39]

The law has been defined as "a set of rules for conduct prescribed by a controlling authority and having binding legal force" (*Black's Law Dictionary* http://en.wikipedia.org/wiki/Black's_Law_ Dictionary). The overriding concern is: What are the beliefs of the controlling authority? Sadly, some public servants, including the vain professors, do not respect the fact that government gets its power from the sovereigns, the taxpayers who created the government and pay their salaries.

How, then, can the people protect themselves from cavalier authoritarians who manipulate changes in laws that enable radicals to dumb down students and, by extension, over time manipulate society?

Historians Will and Ariel Durant pointed out Solon of Athens' recognition of the critical procedural choice that is directly related to limiting the options for political deception. Do we insist upon "government by written and permanent law," or do we permit "government by incalculable and changeable decrees?"[40]

Impressions of Solon of Athens and other lawmakers from different cultures, with the focus on Moses and the Ten Commandments, are displayed on the Supreme Court building in Washington, DC. Although Solon did not support his understanding with references to the Old Testament for reliable standards, he did recognize the ongoing dangers of deception by authoritarians who manage to dominate soft sciences.

"Government by written and permanent law" is not complicated. No matter what one's religion, birthright, or political view, the principles of the *Declaration* and universal absolutes shown here clearly distinguish right from wrong: Stealing property that belongs to another is violating an unalienable right upon which liberty depends. Adultery is a violation of the sacred obligations of marriage and family. Adultery creates stress and shortens life. Dishonesty cheats the victim out of an unalienable, God-given right and undermines the reliable communication upon which commerce and community depend. Deliberately stopping the heart of an unborn child is a horrific offense to the God of life as well as to society.

William Ellery Channing wrote: "Erase all thought and fear of God from a community, and selfishness and sensuality would absorb the whole man. Appetite knowing no restraint, and poverty and suffering having no solace or hope, man would trample in scorn on the restraints of human laws. Virtue, duty, principle would be mocked and scorned as unmeaning sounds. A sordid self-interest would supplant every feeling, and man would become … a companion of brutes."[41]

"Government by written and permanent law" provides long-term stability. Mankind is protected from short-lived popular fantasies and preserved from the inroads of political deception. Secular elitists who insist that the American charter for the use of government power is a "living constitution" now artfully advance "government by incalculable and changeable decrees." To retain respect for the family and liberty, the *Constitution* must be anchored to the political truth adopted by the Founding Fathers.

CHAPTER 6
Defilement of the Judiciary

Previously we have reviewed the exciting history of American foundations that has been omitted from public school textbooks. In this chapter, we seek to answer the question, "Why is it that so many things have gone wrong in the judicial branch of the federal government?"

Before proceeding, we want to acknowledge and honor the many attorneys and truly fine judges, including conservatives, on the Supreme Court who recognize the limited purpose of government and seek to uphold the people as sovereigns under God over government.

Definite and specific American principles for law do exist. Under the influence of these principles, our nation became the overwhelming choice of immigrants throughout the world. Chief among the foundations of the American philosophy for governing is the belief that man is the beneficiary of human rights that are superior to secular claims, government, and things material.

Turning to the *Constitution*: all tools that deliver power—automobiles, atom bombs, governments, and so forth—must have a moral predicate to guide their use. The automobile has a steering wheel, accelerator, and brake pedal that enable man to guide the tool for achieving a desired destination. Speed limits, turning rules, and stop signs are the predicate, the morally significant basis for safe travel. Success is assured if the driver is educated to be responsible and to avoid pitfalls.

The nuts and bolts of the *Constitution* as a tool are specific. The power of government flows from the mammoth equivalent of a local Main-Street bank, the taxpayer-funded public treasury. Even small. privately owned banks need the system of checks to minimize theft by employees and making bad loans. For this same reason, many obstacles and checks were written into the *Constitution*.

Beyond the need for internal protection of the public treasury is the need for the principles of the Creator-based *Declaration of Independence*, later expanded and codified for the citizens' *Bill of Rights*. The first ten amendments (citizens' *Bill of Rights*) are the predicate for steering government power and using the public treasury in ways that will not interfere with man's "unalienable rights" and industry.

In his Farewell Address to the nation, President Washington said: "Towards the preservation of your government, and the permanency of your present happy state, it is requisite, not only that you steadily discountenance irregular oppositions to its acknowledged authority, but also that you resist with care the spirit of innovation upon its principles, however specious the pretexts. One method of assault may be to effect, in the forms of the *Constitution*, alterations which will impair the energy of the system, and thus to undermine what cannot be directly overthrown" (http://avalon.law.yale.edu/18th_century/washing.asp).

Washington continues, expressing what has proven to be very important: **"If, in the opinion of the people, the distribution or modification of the constitutional powers be in any particular wrong, let it be corrected by an amendment in the way which the *Constitution* designates. But let there be no change by usurpation; for though this, in one instance, may be the instrument of good, it is the customary weapon by which free governments are destroyed. The precedent must always greatly overbalance in permanent evil any partial or transient benefit, which the use can at any time yield."**

Liberals in our midst understand the value of stealthful cradle-to-grave government (socialism) as a tool for subduing, ruling, and exploiting the people. What they object to is the impartial Creator-based principles, the absolutes for constitutional law that keep government on the side of citizen self-rule for liberty. "If we and our posterity reject religious instruction and authority, violate the rules of eternal justice, trifle with the injunctions of morality [allow leftist secular militants to dictate what students are taught], and recklessly destroy the ... Constitution which holds us together, no man can tell how sudden a catastrophe may overwhelm us that shall bury our glory in profound obscurity" (Daniel Webster, January 18, 1782–October 24, 1852, an attorney and statesman who argued several cases before the John Marshall court).[42]

"The law given from Sinai was civil and municipal as well as a moral and religious code; it contained many statutes ... of universal application—laws essential to the existence of men in society, and most of which have been enacted by every nation which ever professed any code of laws" (John Quincy Adams, the sixth president of the United States).[43]

Federalism is fundamental to American jurisprudence. Distribution of authority consistent with the laws of creation's nature is needed to facilitate harmony among the states in such matters as interstate commerce, transportation, foreign policy, and national defense. This protects the nation as a whole. The central government, however, was not to get involved in domestic policy unless there was a trend in a region of the country that threatened the unity and survival of the nation as a whole. Because needs within individual states, counties, and cities differ and are better resolved locally, the right to make such laws belongs to the individual states and local citizens. Failure of legislators and judges to respect the superior value of local control in domestic matters leads to a citizen-to-government disconnect and the tyranny of centralized authoritarian rule.

Failure of public schools to teach respect for "In God We Trust," along with the self-evident laws of creation's nature, and emphasize the principles of the *Declaration of Independence* raises a pertinent question: "How does this classroom strategy differ from that of the Fascists and the Communists?"

Under the false premise that professors must be independent from citizen guidelines for what students are to be taught in the soft science in order have the freedom to determine and teach the truth, government-employed teachers have been sheltered by tenure laws. This has enabled secular militants to take moral law, which makes limited government and liberty achievable, out of soft sciences curriculums. Consequently small cadres of atheistic teachers bully the good teachers and dumb down American youth. The all-out war against the nonsectarian God of life and liberty is clear.

Where Vocal Leaders
in the Judiciary Went Terribly Wrong

What was the tactic of liberals in academia and on the Supreme Court that corrupted the functionality of the judiciary and caused havoc in America?

I. The Highest Court in the Land Is Not the Supreme Authority.

The reckless attitude of supremacist judges may stem in part from the use of the term "Supreme" Court when naming the highest court in the US judiciary. The Founding Fathers knew that the highest court itself is not the supreme authority. Proof beyond any doubt can be demonstrated by a factual review of American foundations presented in this book.

Dr. Benjamin Franklin's motion for daily prayer at the Constitutional Convention, June 28, 1787, focuses upon the Founding Fathers' beliefs about Supreme Authority:

"In this situation of this Assembly, groping as it were in the dark to find political truth, and scarce able to distinguish it when presented to us, how has it happened, Sir, that we have not hitherto once thought of humbly applying to the Father of lights to illuminate our understandings? In the beginning of the Contest with Great Britain, when we were sensible of danger we had daily prayer in this room for the divine protection. Our prayers, Sir, were heard, and they were graciously answered… . I have lived, Sir, a long time, and the longer I live, the more convincing proofs I see of this truth—that God governs in the affairs of men. And if a sparrow cannot fall to the ground without his notice, is it probable that an empire can rise without his aid? We have been assured, Sir, in the sacred writings, that "except the Lord build the House they labor in vain that build it." I firmly believe this; and I also believe that without his concurring aid we shall succeed in this political building no better than the Builders of Babel: We shall be divided by our little partial local interests; our projects will be confounded, and we ourselves shall become a reproach and bye word down to future ages.

"I therefore beg leave to move—that henceforth prayers imploring the assistance of Heaven, and its blessings on our deliberations, be held in this Assembly every morning before we proceed to business, and that one or more of the clergy of this city be requested to officiate in that service."

Dr. Franklin himself seconded a substitute motion by Edmund Jennings Randolph: "That a sermon be preached at the request of the convention on the 4th of July, the anniversary of Independence; and thenceforward prayers be used in ye Convention every morning." Six days later, the entire assembly of delegates worshiped together, with testimonies of praise to God at a nearby church in Philadelphia (http://www.wallbuilders.com/LIBissuesArticles.asp?id=98).

II. The Creator-Based *Declaration of Independence* is the Moral Predicate for Constitutional Law.

The second related cause of judicial incompetence is the foolishness of judges who have closeted the true role of the nation's basis for law—the Biblical principles of the *Declaration of Independence*.

The rule or "government of laws" occurs when the voting sovereigns base their preferences for government on the wisdom that is available from the Creator and the self-evident boundaries of creation's nature. And then the people elect like-minded representatives to serve as lawmakers. In contrast, self-righteous liberals, especially law professors who are given captive audiences (not held accountable to those who pay their salaries), fool people by teaching them that God *has* no relevance.

Citizens and judges *must* reject the wisdom of creation's God. Then hierarchical elites slip into the vacuum as god, and society experiences the tyranny of the rule or "government of man."

John Marshall, wrote the landmark 1803 *Marbury v. Madison* opinion, that inaugurated the concept of judicial review. He served as chief justice of the Supreme Court from February 4, 1801, to July 4, 1835. Marshall saw the importance of biblical morality in civic affairs as did the other Founding Fathers.

When writing the *Marbury v. Madison* opinion, Marshall said: "The government of the United States has been emphatically termed a government of laws, and not of men.… That the people have an original right to establish, for their future government, such principles as, in their opinion, shall most conduce to their own happiness, is the basis, on which the whole American fabric has been erected. The principles, therefore, so established, are deemed fundamental. And as the authority, from which they proceed, is supreme, and can seldom act, they are designed to be permanent" (http://usa.usembassy.de/etexts/democrac/9.htm).

The meaning and intent of Chief Justice Marshall's statement—"The government of the United States has been emphatically termed a government of laws, and not of men"—is clear. "The government of laws" is based upon impartial Higher Authority moral law, "and not of men." The benefit is that "government of laws, and not of men" is anchored in the timeless principles revealed by Scripture and proven beneficial in the American experience. This stands in contrast to arbitrary rule and oppression that follow governments "of men," meaning rule by privileged authoritarians. Application of this basic understanding preserves the all-important predicate for the safe and impartial application of government power. It is the "rule of law," emphasized by Moses, that identifies with the desirable outcomes that prevail over circumstances and diverse cultural environments.

John Adams also used the words "government of laws, and not of men" when he wrote the *Bill of Rights* for the Massachusetts Constitution in 1780 (www2.bartleby.com/73/991.html). The preamble to the Massachusetts Constitution includes: "We, therefore, the people of Massachusetts, acknowledging, with grateful hearts, the goodness of the great Legislator of the universe, in affording us, in the course of His providence, an opportunity, deliberately and peaceably, without fraud, violence or surprise, of entering into an original, explicit, and solemn compact with each other; and of forming a new constitution of civil government, for ourselves and posterity; and devoutly imploring His direction in so interesting a design, do agree upon, ordain and establish the following Declaration of Rights, and Frame of Government, as the Constitution of the Commonwealth of Massachusetts." The Massachusetts *Bill of Rights* goes on to read like the principles in the Creator-based *Declaration of Independence* (http://www.malegislature. gov/Laws/Constitution#cp00s00.htm).

In contrast, a government "of men" rests upon revisionist morality, which makes the *Constitution* meaningless. Contemporary liberals who reject the God-honoring meaning for "government of laws, and not of men" are aided by militant atheists, who not only reject "government of law," but work feverishly to eliminate all references to God in education and public discourse. Described by Solon of Athens (last paragraph page 71) as "government by incalculable and changeable decrees," the religious justification for revisionist morality is a strongly held belief about life's origin, meaning, and purpose: atheistic Darwinism ("government by incalculable and changeable decrees," Will and Ariel Durant, *The Story of Civilization, Vol. II, The Life of Greece*, Simon and Schuster, 1939, 118). Sold as absolute science, their demand for education exclusivity is, in reality, the religion of scientific fascism. Liberals are constantly revising Darwin's theory because the absurdity of their science is continually being exposed. The underlying cause of the anger and militancy for their demands becomes clear. They must prevent any ideological competition in the taxpayer-funded classroom. Secular militants must have total control in order to dumb the students down.

John Marshall's Higher Authority basis for rejecting the atheistic secular government "of men" also concurs in full with the public standard of Benjamin Franklin whose call for prayer was adopted by the delegates at the Constitutional Convention. In this regard Henry Steele Commager, eminent historian of the twentieth century, points to the Creator-based *Declaration of Independence* as the source of America's unique principles of government, and refers to America's new political system for the vindication of God-given rights as "matchless logic" and of "permanent" rather than "transient" value.[44]

When confronting the greatest crisis since the War for Independence, Abraham Lincoln turned to the *Declaration* to assert the "sacred right of self-government" (Abraham Lincoln, October 10, 1854, Peoria, Illinois (http://www.nps.gov/liho/historyculture/peoriaspeech.htm).

Elected representatives make laws and serve by the "consent of the governed," who are **endowed by their Creator**" with certain unalienable rights. This claim reaches the very heart of American society and law. Conservative Supreme Court justices have cited the *Declaration* as support for their decisions over two hundred times. The *Federalist Papers*, written to promote acceptance of the *Constitution* by the people, cited the *Declaration* thirty-seven times.

Unabashed belief in the providence of the universal and impartial God of creation, as a political principle, is fully American. This was the source of the courage of the Founding Fathers when risking confrontation by the greatest military force on earth at the time. The Higher Authority standard for morality in matters of law is indelibly written in American history: "The Representatives of the United States of America, in General Congress, Assembled, appealing to the Supreme Judge of the world for the rectitude of our intentions ... And for the support of this *Declaration* [of Independence], with a firm reliance on the protection of Divine Providence, we mutually pledge to each other our Lives, our Fortunes, and our sacred Honor."

III. The Intended Meaning of the *Constitution,* Altered and Twisted by the Politicalization of *Marbury v. Madison.*

The great harm done to America by liberal judges is, in no small part, due to the shameless contrivance and exploitation of the *Marbury v.*

Madison decision. It was not the intent of the *Marbury v. Madison* decision to make the court supreme and enable judges to assume the role of the people's representatives and make law or to be administrators of the law. The court settled a dispute as prescribed by the *Constitution*. Liberals who believe that unelected judges have the right to originate laws or step in and be administrators in non-court administration matters demonstrate an immoral and titanic supremacist violation of the Constitutional separation of powers.

Repeating the words of Chief Justice John Marshall: "The government of the United States has been emphatically termed a government of laws, and not of men.… That the people have an original right to establish, for their future government, such principles as, **in their opinion, shall most conduce to their own happiness, is the basis on which the whole American fabric has been erected. The principles … are deemed fundamental. And as the authority, from which they proceed, is supreme … they are designed to be permanent**" (http://usa.usembassy.de/etextsdemocrac/9.htm).

John Marshall endured the freezing winter at Valley Forge as a soldier in the Third Virginia Regiment in the War for Independence. He risked his life to enforce the moral absolutes as the predicate for law outlined in the *Declaration of Independence*.

Further proof of Chief Justice Marshall's rejection and avoidance of secular adventurism in *Marbury v. Madison* is his letter to Jasper Adams, written May 9, 1833, "The American population is entirely Christian, and with us Christianity and Religion are identified. It would be strange indeed, if with such a people, our institutions did not presuppose Christianity, and did not often refer to it, and exhibit relations with it" (http://www.errantskeptics.org/FoundingFathers.htm).

A notable perversion of the purpose of judicial review came fifty years later in the *Dred Scott v. Sandford* opinion. That decision by the court eliminated any doubt about the appetite of some judges for overtaking the role of the people's representatives elected to establish law. The *Dred Scott v. Sandford* decision decreed that black people could not be citizens under the *Constitution* because they were "of an inferior order." What an egregious violation of the Supreme Court's authority! President Abraham Lincoln opposed the decision, and it did not stand as precedent for long.

Ninety years after *Dred Scott v. Sandford* came the 1947 *Everson v. Board of Education* decision. This departure from American legal foundations struck at the very heart of self-government and liberty. Within fifteen years, radicals on American campuses were gleefully rejecting and attacking core American belief for law. **Everson v. Board of Education appears to have been by far the most harmful court action taken against individual liberty since the *Dred Scott v. Sandford* decision.**

The *Everson v. Board of Education* decision twisted the meaning of the First Amendment of the *Constitution* in two ways. "First, the phrase emphasizes separation of church and state—unlike the First Amendment, which speaks in terms of non-establishment and free exercise of religion. Second, a wall [term used by the Court] is a bilateral barrier that inhibits the activities of both civil government and religion—unlike the First Amendment, which imposes restrictions on civil government only [not on religious freedom]."[45]

Thomas Jefferson's "wall of separation" metaphor was totally misrepresented by the judges. He adamantly objected to any such tyranny against religious liberty. Engraved on the Jefferson Memorial in Washington, DC are his own words: "I have sworn upon the altar of God eternal hostility against every form of tyranny over the mind of man." He was a religious seeker and regularly attended church services held on Sundays in the United States Capitol building.[46]

Instead of upholding their oath to abide by the *Constitution*, judges ruled by "incalculable and changeable decrees." Rule by men replaced government by established law. The reasoning behind their decision reflects the old European secular doctrine of open-mindedness for dumbing the people down and transforming society (see Chapter 7). Instead of being umpires, unelected judges are trampling on the sacred rights of the people by legislating superior rights for the enemies of responsible liberty.

The importance of firmness in retaining the original meaning of the *Constitution* for judiciary, legislative, and administrative separation merits repeated emphasis. The duty of unelected judges is to settle disputes based upon the *Constitution* and Precedents consistent with the *Constitution*. Responding to the question, "Is there a role for politics in our judicial system?" Antonin Scalia, who has now served for over twenty years on the Supreme Court, said: "The absolute worst violation of a judge's oath is to decide a case based on a partisan principle or philosophical basis, rather than what the law [states]."[47]

Prior to the *Everson v. Board of Education* decision in 1947, the First Amendment protected religious liberty. Liberals going to court to get the Ten Commandments removed from public property would have been wasting their time. A disruptive student who objects to the statement "Jesus is the reason for the season" on T-shirts in the public school would not have threatened a lawsuit. The force of government was on the side of the people's civic right to use their institutions, including public education, to proclaim belief in the nonsectarian God of creation.

The First Amendment upholds the unalienable right of the people to share their religious beliefs and make comparisons. With this knowledge they can then choose what appears to be best. This competition between the religions strengthens the Higher Authority "government of laws, and not of men" consensus among voters.

"On every question of construction, carry ourselves back to the time when the *Constitution* was adopted, recollect the spirit manifested in the debates, and instead of trying what meaning may be squeezed out of the text, or invented against it, conform to the probable one in which it was passed" (June 12, 1823, Thomas Jefferson, *Autobiography Notes on the State of Virginia, Public and Private Papers, Addresses and Letters,* New York: The Library of America, 1984)."[48]

The limited role of Judges bears repeating:

1. The boundaries of authority that limits the role of judges to settling disputes is mandated by the construct of the *Constitution*. Chief Justice John Roberts, quoted in the previous chapter, compares the role of the judges with the role of baseball umpires. Baseball needs umpires to call balls and strikes, but umpires are never allowed to change the rules in the middle of the game.

2. The umpire illustration is consistent with the *Federalist Papers*. They were written by Alexander Hamilton, James Madison, and John Jay in 1787 and published to encourage the people in the states to ratify the *Constitution*. *Federalist Paper* No. 78 described the judiciary as being the "least dangerous" and "weakest" of the three branches of government because it is the arbitrator of disputes: "The judiciary ... has no influence over either the sword [imposing the penalties advocated by the court] or the purse; no direction either of the strength or the wealth of society, and can take no active resolution whatever. It may truly be said that to have neither force nor will but merely judgment; and must ultimately depend upon the aid of the executive arm for efficacy of its judgments" (http://www.constitution.org/fed/federa78.htm).

3. The *Marbury v. Madison* decision was simply to settle a dispute. Defensive actions by one branch of government over another, meaning separation of powers, is intended by the *Constitution*. On occasion, the court may settle a dispute involving the other branches of government and legislators may and *should* intervene and correct the Supreme Court. Also, the administrative branch may *challenge* the courts to change a court's mandate. The American system is "a Republic—a federation, or combination, of central and state republics—under which: the different governments will control each other.... Within each republic there are two safeguarding features: (a) a division of powers, as well as (b) a system of checks and balances between separate departments [including the judiciary] : hence a double security arises [essential] to the rights of the people" (*Federalist*, No. 51, by James Madison).

4. Chief Justice Marshall in *Marbury v. Madison* stated: "This original and supreme will [of the people] organizes the government, and

assigns, to different departments, their respective powers. It may either stop here; or establish certain limits not to be transcended by those departments. The government of the United States is of the latter description. The powers of the legislature [as well as the judiciary and the administrative] are defined, and limited; and that those limits may not be mistaken, or forgotten, the *Constitution* is written" (http://usa.usembassy.de/etexts/democrac/9.htm).

> The original purpose of judicial review established by the *Marbury v. Madison* decision was certainly NOT to empower judges to become unelected legislators or administrators.

Let's tighten up the language and clear the air. The language of secular open-mindedness, along with Darwinian origin and meaning of life, are diabolical enemies of the rule of law. The underpinning for the rule of law rests in the July 4, 1776, *Declaration* that gave birth to the United States of America. All men "*... are endowed by their Creator with certain unalienable Rights, that among these are Life, Liberty and the pursuit of Happiness. — That to secure these rights, Governments are instituted among Men, deriving their just powers from the consent of the governed, — That whenever any Form of Government becomes destructive of these ends, it is the Right of the People to alter or to abolish it, and to institute new Government, laying its foundation on such principles and organizing its powers in such form, as to them shall seem most likely to effect their Safety and Happiness.*" Appellate court judges need not bow down to atheistic secular legalese. The impartial non-sectarian Supreme role of a Higher Authority, emphasized in the *Declaration,* is justifiably appropriate when writing a court opinion.

It is needful that we reject the spirit of rebellion and enjoin the spirit of truth that empowers man to storm the strongholds of evil. It is spiritual wisdom that enabled this nation to become the most blessed civilization in history. The restoration of spiritual glory—the potential to reassert our culture's values of freedom, education, prosperity, and truth—is at hand.

Using twisted renderings of the *Bill of Rights*, leftist lawyers and tenured radicals in education have forced Americans—good teachers, as well as the citizen majority—into submission. They terrorize by denigrating the reputation of teachers who dare to disagree and endangering the financial solvency of those who must hire expensive lawyers to defend traditional American values. Secular militants have shut down ideological competition by preventing religious, political, and academic freedom on many campuses throughout the nation. Haters of citizen self-government in America are effectively muting the voices of tens of millions of concerned citizens.

The war against the Judeo-Christian foundation for American law, self-government, and the spirit of liberty extends beyond their censorship of American history and foundational American beliefs from public school textbooks. "A decorated pine tree in the Ames High School cafeteria has been taken down because of complaints from a high school employee and some parents" (*The Tribune*, December 4, 2010). Reporting the words of the school Superintendent, "We are in the business of educating students. I didn't want this [decorated pine tree] to become a distraction ... So we decided it would be best to take down the tree." His frankness, about a few people who were intolerant of a pine tree within the sight of students is commendable. The tree was in the school for the traditional Christmas season, but apparently they dared not even call it a Christmas tree.

No nation, however great, can withstand the politicization of the soft sciences that comes with the establishment of teacher union tenure laws. "All power tends to corrupt, and absolute power corrupts absolutely."[49]

Phyllis Schlafly's *The Supremacists: The Tyranny of Judges and How to Stop It*, published in 2004, documents scores of devastating decisions that flow directly or indirectly from the exploitation and contrivance of *Marbury v. Madison* and the *Everson v. Board of Education* precedents (examples starting with the Warren Court below). The harm is compounded by neglect of the Tenth Amendment, which places the authority over laws with the states, counties, and cities according to the will of the local body politic: "The powers not delegated to the United

States by the *Constitution*, nor prohibited by it to the States, are reserved to the States respectively, or to the people."[50]

The harm that has resulted from the activist Earl Warren Court (Supreme Court 1953–69) is beyond measure. The citizens' *Bill of Rights* was not intended to leverage by law the lies and subterfuge of the Communists or other ideological supremacists. Perhaps the greatest damage has been the loss of quality education taught unabashedly by pro-family, pro-life, and pro-American teachers. Good teachers simply submit or leave the profession. The soft sciences in schools saddled by tenure laws are not the only victim. Student abilities in the hard sciences have suffered (http://www.chron.com/disp/story.mpl/nation/7327936.html).

"On August 7, 1957, the Senate Subcommittee on Internal Security held a hearing on the 'Limitation of Appellate Jurisdiction of the United States Supreme Court' [arising from decisions by the Warren Court] at which Senator William E. Jenner testified: 'There was a time when the Supreme Court conceived its function to be the interpretation of the law. For some time now, the Supreme Court has been making law— substituting its judgment for the judgment of the legislative branch. We witness today the spectacle of a Court constantly changing the law, and even changing the meaning of the *Constitution*, in an apparent determination to make the law of the land what the Court thinks it should be.' Echoing the testimony of others, Senator Jenner continued: 'The Senate was wrong. The House of Representatives was wrong. The Secretary of State was wrong. The Department of Justice was wrong. The State legislatures were wrong. The State courts were wrong. The prosecutors, both Federal and State, were wrong. The juries were wrong. The Federal Bureau of Investigation was wrong. The Loyalty Review Board was wrong. The New York Board of Education was wrong. The California bar examiners were wrong.… The Ohio Committee on Un-American Activities was wrong. Everybody was wrong except the attorneys for the Communist conspiracy and the majority of the United States Supreme Court'" (Phyllis Schlafly, *The Supremacists: The Tyranny of Judges and How to Stop It*, Dallas, TX: Spence Publishing Company, 2004, p. 108. This highly recommended book may be purchased at http://www.eagleforum.org/order/book).

Following is additional documentation from *The Supremacists: The Tyranny of Judges and How to Stop It*:

1945–47 (pages 105–6, 155–59, 175) Laws protecting Americans from fraudulent disinformation about Communists working in America were overturned. This, in large part, has led to the arrogance of radical professors and the radicalization of students starting in the 1960s. Many of these students are now teaching in lower-level, taxpayer-funded government schools throughout America.

1953 (pages 17–34) Judges make war against public acclaim of God, the Pledge of Allegiance, the Ten Commandments, and prayer.

1964 (pages 76–81) Liberal judges cripple law enforcement.

1966 (pages 57–64) Judges overturn laws prohibiting the marketing of pornography.

1973 (pages 65–75) Judges adopt the radical feminist agenda, requiring all state legislators to accept the legalization of abortion in *Roe v. Wade*.

1985 (pages 92–96) Judges assume the authority as judges to impose taxes on the public.

1993 (pages 35–46) Judges war against marriage and the family, established and upheld for thousands of years.

1999 (pages 47–56) Judges undermine US sovereignty by paying deference to the agendas and laws of foreign nations, including laws that prohibit capital punishment and give the citizen franchise to felons.

2003 (pages 69 and 141) Liberal judges attack the Boy Scouts and other gender-specific organizations.

Resting upon legal precedents reaching back to 1945, the American Civil Liberties Union and leftist teacher union bosses are reaching beyond their control of public education to war against God and American values elsewhere. For example, the Teachers [Union] Association of California spent $1.25 million in opposition to a Proposition 8 amendment that supported the marriage between one man and one woman. That $1.25 million came from teachers' union dues. According to Reg Weaver, outgoing president of the National Education Association, one-third of the NEA union members are Republicans and one-third are Independents. "Each California teacher pays $922 each year in California Teachers Association dues" (*Los Angeles Times*, November 18, 2008, cited by the *November Education Reporter*, St. Louis, Missouri).

As long as the court fails to restore the First Amendment, intended to prevent, among other things, establishment of government employment guarantees, radical government teachers will continue to rip into the moral fabric of the American mind. The Ten Commandments, featured on the walls of the US Supreme Court Building, will continue to be found and removed from schools and other public buildings throughout the nation. Although this is being vigorously protested, American foundations in God honoring faith was largely absent from the new Visitor Center that has now become a gateway to the Capitol Building in Washington, DC. Even the words "religion and morality" were stripped from the education mandate of the *Northwest Ordinance* displayed in the Visitor Center (http://christianactionleague.org/new/war-on-god-in-america/).

Stare decisis is no excuse for preserving bad court precedent. *Stare decisis* is legal talk for an everyday practice that we all follow. It simply means that once a decision is implemented, it should be supported for a considerable period of time to see if, in fact, it is helping or, at a minimum, not doing harm. The practice of preserving court precedent was never intended to be a mandate for national suicide.

Judge Robert Bork observed that the courts, and especially the Supreme Court, have become "the enemy of traditional culture," in areas including "speech, religion, abortion, sexuality, welfare, public education and much else." He continued, "It is not too much to say that the suffocating vulgarity of popular culture is in large measure the work of the Court."[51]

PART II:
Education

Chapters 7 to 10

"Be it remembered, however, that liberty must at all hazards be supported ... cannot be preserved without a general knowledge among the people ... And the preservation of the means of knowledge among the lowest ranks, is of more importance to the public than all the property of all the rich men in the country. The people ... have a right, from the frame of their nature, to knowledge, as their great Creator, who does nothing in vain, has given them understandings, and a desire to know."

From the 1765 "Dissertation on the Canon and Feudal Law," by John Adams. He was a devout Christian, a Harvard-educated lawyer, and a delegate to the First and Second Continental Congresses that adopted the Declaration of Independence. *He was the second president of the United States. Adams's wife, Abigail, has been recognized as a Founding Mother because of her influence on behalf of women's rights. Their son, John Quincy Adams, was the sixth president of the United States.*

CHAPTER 7
Academic Freedom and Teacher Tenure History

This chapter is introduced with a question: "Is it coincidental that both the moral standards and test scores of students have declined precipitously with the secularization of education?"

Teacher tenure law was brought from Europe to America with the founding of the American Association of University Professors in 1915. Their first president, Professor John Dewey (1859–1952), was a published atheist. Dewey reminded conferees, "To have failed to undertake these initial demands would have been cowardly."[52]

The abuse of academic freedom and teacher tenure guarantees is rooted in the old European secular philosophy. John S. Brubacher and Willis Rudy point out that, when Darwinian advocates coupled their "origin and destiny of man" theory with the authoritarianism of "German graduate methods [faculty independence] ... academic freedom became a cause celebre [highly controversial]."[53] According to Darwinian militants, "There is no fixed limit or perfect form of knowledge and, that on the contrary, truth is always tentative."[54]

The harmful impact of teacher tenure guarantees arises from the use of law (government power) to shelter teachers from accountability to the public for what they teach. "The obligations of the teacher are direct to truth, and the teacher who, in order to please anybody, suppresses important information, or says things he knows are not true, or refrains from saying things that need to be said in the interest of truth, betrays his calling and renders himself unworthy to belong to the company of teachers."[55]

John Dewey is recognized as a key leader of the Teachers Union, Local 5, which was organized in 1916 as an affiliate of the American Federation of Teachers (AFT) in New York City. The union's principal target was the repeal of the Lusk Laws, statutes that allowed for the revocation of a teacher's license "if he is not of good moral character—or if by act or utterance he shows that he will not support the *Constitution* of the State or of the United States of America."[56]

This belligerent breed of social engineers gradually pushed its way into the leadership of government-administered education. The group also included Professor John Dewey, the first president of the American Association of University Professors (AAUP), and Dewey was one of the signers of the first *Humanist Manifesto*. He also served as honorary president of the National Education Association (NEA) after it came under leftist control.

As we shall see, authoritarians demand taxpayer-funded tenure guarantees as the means to finance and empower their war against citizen self-rule and liberty. To achieve their goal, they must have the freedom to turn the minds of students away from the beliefs of their parents and traditional American values.

Those who champion the atheistic-secular concept of open-mindedness use it to justify exclusivity for imposing their God-rejecting lifeview upon captive classroom students. "Not only must school teachers and principals be 'exemplars of open-mindedness and free inquiry, but severally and collectively, they must be prepared to proclaim their faith in that open-mindedness and free inquiry.' Here we must hearken to Dewey: 'The administrator will ... realize that public education is essentially education of the public: directly, through teachers and students ... in the transformation of society [into an atheistic socialistic society].'"[57]

Atheistic-secular demands that "school teachers and principals be exemplars of open-mindedness [in] the transformation of society" undermine the moral foundations of civil society. The justification for a tax on the people for education, in a representative republic, requires that the curriculum promote foundational moral boundaries. The Constitutions of the Soviet Union, China, and Cuba proclaimed liberty. But in the absence of a moral predicate providing certainties for Constitutional law—such as provided in the American *Declaration of Independence* and *Northwest Ordinance,* they rule by what Solon of Athens called "incalculable and changeable decrees."[58]

Prior to the leftist takeover, the National Education Association had published God-honoring, character-building booklets for students and parents as recently as 1950. For example, *A Golden Treasury from the Bible,* Personal Growth Leaflet contained twenty-four Bible verses, including Psalm 1; Proverbs 20:1; Exodus 20 (the Ten Commandments); Romans 12; John 3:16, 6:23, 14:1–4, and 15:1–4; 1 Corinthians 13; and Ecclesiastes 12:1, "Remember now thy Creator in the days of thy youth."

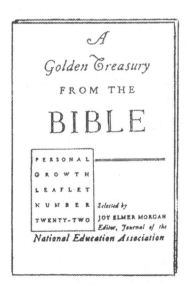

In contrast to the old European secular philosophy, the American philosophy of education requires that all prominent views, including the atheistic-secular view, be introduced, but that they are to be taught in the context of the history of their outcomes! This is seen in the resolution proposed by both Thomas Jefferson and James Madison and adopted by the newly founded University of Virginia (see Chapter 10). Their resolution identifies the great need of our day, stressing citizen responsibility and the need for a thorough knowledge of historic American foundations.

The education guidelines set forth for the University of Virginia emphasize that "all students shall be 'inculcated' with the basic American principles of government," and, "None should be inculcated which are incompatible with those on which the *Constitution* of this State, and of the United States were genuinely based, in the common opinion." The resolution also stated that the faculty had a standard of responsibility and were required to teach affirmatively these unique American principles. Only after they had done so were they to teach the conflicting principles as such, judging them by the soundness of the American principles that served as a basis.[59] These principles are detailed in Chapter 10 of this book, and also at http://faculty. virginia. edu/villagespaces/essay/ "Education That Is Profoundly American."

Faithful school boards and administrators take seriously the fact that youthful trust, inexperience, and vulnerability to exploitation by the enemies of the family and self-government require that the learning environment be protected. God has given mankind a wonderful mind to use and explore the universe, with but one exception: we are not to use our minds to absorb the details and wiles (deceptive snares) of evil (Gen. 3:13; Isa. 5:15–16, 20; Rom. 16:19; and James 1:12–17).

The collective political power of teacher unions, established by legislative and judicial approval, has enabled them to prevent curriculum control by elected school boards and superintendents hired to administer the system. Not surprising, an Ames, Iowa, public school board member complained: "I know the Legislature likes to talk about local control, but what I am getting [at] is that … we really don't have local control."[60] The direct harm of tenure laws in the hard sciences (math, engineering, chemistry, physics, and so forth) is much less than in the soft sciences. Whether or not the researcher or teacher is a Bible-believer, the conclusions drawn in the hard sciences tend to be the same because proof is determined by observing consistently repeatable and immutable laws of creation's nature. Misrepresentations are typically exposed and rejected as a result of our free enterprise system, which thrives on competition and the consumer's right to choose from products that come from the hard sciences.

In contrast, conclusions drawn in the soft sciences—such as literature, news editing, education strategies, political science, life-origins biology, history, law, social studies, arts, and ecology—differ starkly between creationist and evolutionist instructors. The differences include the acceptance or rejection of moral certainties, an honest or dishonest rendition of history, and respect or disregard for parental authority and for the *Constitution* itself. When an evolutionist instructs a student year after year, the student's ability to separate truth from non-truth and to appreciate the value of moral law and the traditional family becomes seriously impaired.

The Supreme Court's failure to apply the First Amendment for its intended purposes destroyed the perimeters necessary for the law to protect society from morally incompetent teachers. Statewide public sector collective bargaining laws, enabling tenure guarantees for unqualified teachers, crept silently into legislation for lower-level public schools beginning in the early 1970s. Only seven states have rejected such laws for teachers. The leftist NEA union advantage for control proceeds, however, without tenure laws in those seven states.

Two paragraphs for teacher contracts demanded by NEA unions are the root of the problem. These controlling paragraphs may be found in the contract between the NEA union (or its state affiliate) and the local school board or in the state public sector collective bargaining laws. One paragraph provides teacher tenure, which makes it virtually impossible to fire a teacher. Secondly, a confidentiality paragraph makes it a crime for school administrators to disclose the reasons for dismissing a teacher without judicial approval—a very costly and lengthy procedure. If the citizens are not permitted by law to be informed, the political support from the citizens, so desperately needed by the superintendent in order to fire a bad teacher, is kept in check.

"Precisely because of the obvious potential for abuse, even labor union advocates like AFL-CIO President George Meany and Franklin D. Roosevelt viewed unionization of the public employees as unthinkable."[61]

In March 2008, harsh debate in the Iowa legislature brought this problem to the public's attention. Radicals, whose elections were advanced by large sums of campaign money received from outside the state, were pushing for changes in the public sector collective bargaining law. A section making it even harder to fire harmful teachers caused "grave concerns" among school administrators. "Margaret Buckton, chief lobbyist for the Iowa Association of School Boards, says [arbitration] adjudicators have tended to rule in favor of the teachers." As the teachers' bargaining rights law now stands, "Attempts to remove a teacher can last years and cost hundreds of thousands of dollars."[62]

Any force that makes it impossible for the school administrator to be in control and implement the citizen consensus for values is, by definition, fascistic and advances the consequences of Fascism. It was this ever-present threat and its consequent tyranny of the mind that prompted elected representatives in the individual states to require that First Amendment curbs be placed upon government employees and added to the federal *Constitution*.

Much maligned by leftists, there are several studies that document the way that radicals bully their way into control of the social, political, and religious atmosphere on school campuses (even several seminaries). Three excellent books on the subject are *Masters of Deceit*[a] by J. Edgar Hoover, *Chronology of Education with Quotable Quotes*[b] by D. L. Cuddy, and *You Can Still Trust the Communists … to Be Communists (Socialists and Progressives Too)*[c] by Fred C. Schwarz and David A. Noebel.[63]

According to the *Wall Street Journal,* January 3, 2006, the NEA and their unions spent approximately $80.5 million in the 2004–05 school year.

"The NEA gave $65 million of its members' dues to liberal groups last year." Undoubtedly the biggest benefactors, legislative candidates who were willing to promote NEA union power, received over $40 million of those funds. In the 2007–08 year, the NEA national headquarters took in $337.7 million in dues and agency fees.[64]

Myron Lieberman, an educational consultant who recently served as a visiting scholar at Bowling Green University, has emerged as a leading education free-market analyst. He estimates that "the collective bargaining process itself imposes direct and indirect costs that may run into the billions of dollars." According to his book *Public Education: An Autopsy*, "As long as schools remain a government monopoly, cost and quality will be as bad as cost and quality everywhere under socialism."[65] Lieberman is also the author of *The Teachers' Unions: How the NEA and AFT Sabotage Reform and Hold Students, Parents, Teachers, and Taxpayers Hostage to Bureaucracy.*

The dogmatic secular brand of academic freedom and old European atheistic-secular philosophy go hand in hand. It was the collective capacity of unions to raise and distribute money to like minded organizations that was infamously used by the Fascists to corrupt the political process in Italy prior to World War II.

As the education in a nation goes, so goes the nation.

CHAPTER 8
Consequences of the Unionization of Government Teachers

New generations of Americans are being cheated. "Leftist indoctrination is stripping the nation of future leaders and subjecting millions of vulnerable young women and men to physical and mental harm. Statistics concerning disease and related health risks on campuses are staggering."[66]

The atheistic-secular philosophy in the classrooms enforced over the objections of taxpayers poses the greatest single threat, an internal threat, to American society. The greatest threat to American society is not worldwide terrorism. Although it is deceptively presented in textbooks, the determination of leftist authoritarians to destroy moral faith and undermine support for traditional American principles is freely admitted in their own publications. C. F. Potter, a cosigner of the first *Secular Humanist Manifesto* along with John Dewey, writes for his colleagues: "Education is thus a most powerful ally of humanism, and every American public school is a school of humanism. What can the theistic Sunday schools, meeting for an hour once a week, teaching only a fraction of the children, do to stem the tide of a five-day program of humanistic teaching?" (Charles F. Potter, "Humanism: A New Religion," 1930, http://www.allaboutphilosophy.org /secular-humanism.htm).

The following points reflect the mind-altering nature of the ideology and campus culture that a few tenured academians are imposing upon new generations of American students.

1. Eliminating God—They proclaim to be patriots but reject the historic, constitutional right of students to debate and disagree on moral grounds. As a result, some students lose the capacity to make moral decisions.
2. Eliminating truth—They present the moral value of truth as evil and evil as good.
3. Removing traditional values from classroom studies—They seek to destroy belief in sexual virtue and the traditional marriage of one man and one woman.
4. Exalting leaders on the secular left—They praise champions of the culture of dependency and atheistic-secular exclusivity.
5. Encouraging sin by romanticizing feel-good emotions—Secular handlers will not allow anything to be denounced as "sin." Victims self-destruct, wondering why.
6. Glorifying death—They promote suicide, abortion, euthanasia, and lifestyles that shorten life.

Studies show that a high percent of children from Christian families are severely impacted by twelve years of atheistic-secular double-talk (Allan Bloom, *The Closing of the American Mind*, Simon and Schuster: New York, 1993).

American Judeo-Christian Values Compared to
the Old European Secular Philosophy

"In God We Trust"	**God Rejecting Secularism**
American Principles	Contemporary Liberalism
History-Based Predictability	Revisionist History
Moral Truth is Absolute	Revisionist Morality
Stability, Rule of Law	Exploitation, Rule of Man
Government by Written and Permanent Law	Government by Incalculable and Changeable Decree
Laws Anchored by the *Constitution*	The *Constitution* Is Treated As A Political Document

Religious and Political Ideas Open to Competition	Religious and Political Ideas Imposed by Tenured Leftists
Decisions by and for the People Through Their Elected Representatives	Decisions by Tenured Government Authoritarians
Wages Result from Skills, Supply and Product Demand	Wages Controlled by Established Union Monopoly
Limited Government, Taxes Kept Low	Oppressive Government, Indulgent Taxation
Only Criminals Who by The Citizen's Consensus Are Violating God-Given Individual Rights or Commit Other Crimes against Society Are Punished	People Determined by Authoritarians to Be in Violation of the Secular Agenda for Social Engineering Are Isolated Politically and Punished
Spirit of Liberty—Hard Work and Self-Reliance Spiritual Continuity Youth and Immigrants Must Be Educated to Appreciate the Above	Responsibility Relinquished to Collectivist Authoritarians Destroy Spiritual Continuity Keep the People in Fear, and Dumbed Down, Proud, and Secular
LIBERTY	TYRANNY

Perhaps the most virulent among the education strategists in American universities and colleges are the Marxists. Without the senseless intrusion, collective bargaining authority for unions, and teacher tenure laws, Marxism could never have become rooted in public education.

The five paragraphs checked below are from the book *Understanding the Times* by Dr. David A. Noebel, published by Harvest House Publishers, Manitou Springs, Colorado, in 1999, pages 19–20. Citation sources detailed in the book are listed in parentheses.

√ "The strides made by Marxism at American universities in the last two decades are breathtaking," says New York University's Herbert London. He reports that two self-declared "Marxist historians, Eugene Genovese and William A. Williams, were elected presidents of the Organization of American Historians in successive elections. Louis Kampf, a radical with Marxist predilections, was elected president of the Modern Languages Association" (Herbert London).

√ "The field of American history has come to be dominated by Marxists and feminists" (Dr. Arnold Beichman and Professor John P. Diggens, *Accuracy in Academia Campus Report*, July/August 1987).

√ "Marxist academics are today's power elite in the universities" (Georgie Anne Geyer, "Marxism Thrives on Campuses," a *Denver Post* article, quoted by Arnold Beichman, August 29, 1989, B7).

√ "The complexion of education in everything from genetics to sociology and psychology has become decidedly, materialistic" (Malachi Martin, *The Keyes of This Blood*, "The Rising Tide of Marxists' Interpretation of History, Law, Religion and Scientific Inquiry," 262).

√ It is believed that there are at least "ten thousand Marxist professors on America's campuses" (David B. Richardson, "Marxism in US Classrooms," *US News and World Report*, January 25, 1982, 42–45).

The byproduct of the extremes in old European secular philosophy, Marxist influence, currently known as "Left Eclecticism," has reached alarming heights in universities, colleges, and public grade schools in America. Roger Kimball is a highly regarded analyst and writer on the subject of Left Eclecticism. His analysis focuses, in part, on neo-Marxism, which has morphed into structuralism, poststructuralism, Lacanian analysis, deconstruction, women's studies, black studies, gay studies, critical legal studies, new historicism, cultural studies, and Afrocentrism. Marxists have also penetrated liberal church seminaries via liberation theology and social action materialism.[67]

The power of leftist indoctrination on the minds of law students who become judges explains the ignominy of judges that would refuse to ban Marxist doctrine and other one-sided secular literature from taxpayer public schools but would ban reading of the Ten Commandments and make prayer in public schools unlawful, and overturn anti-abortion laws in all fifty states in violation of the Tenth Amendment.

Under three presidents, our nation committed itself to stopping the takeover of Vietnam by the Communists in the north. Over 56,000 Americans died in that war, and the concluding Tet counteroffensive waged by our military was an overwhelming success. But in those few weeks, we lost the war politically, as a result of leftist propaganda and compliant politicians who would not preserve that victory by helping to fund the South Vietnam military.

While most Republican party leaders have resisted the idea of moral relativism, the moral tradition of leaders in the Democrat party is being hijacked. Democrat party leaders in the era of President Harry Truman would never have sanctioned abortion, homosexuality, or same sex marriage.

Measured by political scientists since 1992, atheists have become a growing component of the Democrat party leadership.[68]

Legislative majorities in the Democrat party have repeatedly obstructed government by and for the people. They have applied a leftist litmus test and blocked the people's representatives' right to vote for conservative judge nominees who would support the original meaning of the *Constitution*. Liberal extremists only allow a vote on judge nominees who have a history of compromising the *Constitution*.

America's youth can be compared to the casualties of military conquest. They have become victims of ruinous lifestyles by the millions, and many have actually become troopers in support of leftist political agenda. What is this victimization by education radicals who are sheltered by tenure law if not robbery, blatant betrayal, and treason?

CHAPTER 9
The Education Nightmare

The 1910 US Census Bureau reported that illiteracy (those unable to read) among ten- to twenty-year-olds was down from 7.6 percent in 1900 to 4.7 percent (Dr. Dennis L. Cuddy, *Chronology of Education*, Highland City, FL: Pro Family Forum, Inc., 1993, 12).

Milton and Rose Friedman pointed out in their book *Free to Choose*, published in 1980, that "The education, or rather the uneducation, of [all children in public schools but most harmfully] black children from low income families … [is a] disaster area in education and its most devastating failure." The Friedmans continue: "More than four decades ago Walter Lippmann diagnosed it as 'the sickness of an over-governed society,' … the exercise of un-limited power by men with limited minds and self-regarding prejudices is soon oppressive, reactionary, and corrupt,… that there are no limits to a man's capacity to govern others and that, therefore, no limits ought to be imposed upon government … For schools, this has taken the form of denying many parents control over the kind of schooling their children receive."[69]

The radical minority boastfully proclaims their authoritarian credentials and warns opponents that "Sixty-seven countries' national academy of sciences (including the US National Academy of Science) signed the Inter-academy Panel's Statement on the Teaching of Evolution." The truth is that it was a radical minority in those countries that have "signed" the document.[70]

Albert Einstein (1879–1955) was not stamped by the Darwinian craze. He is thought to be among the most highly revered scientists of the twentieth century. Although not a Christian, he recognized the impossibility of a non-created universe. The *Encyclopedia Britannica* says of Einstein: "Firmly denying atheism, Einstein expressed a belief in 'Spinoza's God who reveals himself in the harmony of what exists.' He once remarked to a young physicist: 'I want to know how God created this world, I am not interested in this or that phenomenon, in the spectrum of this or that element. I want to know His thoughts, the rest are details.' Einstein's famous epithet on the 'uncertainty principle' was 'God does not play dice.' A famous saying of his was 'Science without religion is lame, religion without science is blind'" (For more details search Famous scientists who Believed in God.)

The pseudoscience of evolution rests on Darwin's book *Origin of the Species*. Darwin's theory about the origin of life is both unprovable and illogical. Dr. Soren Lovtrup, a non-Biblicist scientist and author, declares: "Believe that one day the Darwinian myth will be ranked the greatest deceit in the history of science."[71]

This struggle within our educational system is not a debate between science and religion, but between religion and religion, atheism and theism. Science is simply the sphere in which the debate is taking place.

Dr. Michael Ruse, a leading evolutionist and authority on philosophy, points out in his recently published book *The Evolution-Creation Struggle* that the "theory of evolution is, in fact, religion."[72] Dr. Ruse also writes: "Evolution is promoted by its practitioners as more than mere science. Evolution is an ideology, a secular religion, a full-fledged alternative to Christianity with meaning and morality. Evolution is a religion. This was true of evolution in the beginning and is true of evolution today."[73]

Adam Sedgwick, one of Charles Darwin's professors at Cambridge University, took immediate issue with Darwin's book *Origin of the Species*. Sedgwick told his former student that it "greatly shocked my moral taste" and elaborated in a passage that proved prophetic: "There is a moral or metaphysical part of nature as well as a physical. A man who denies this is deep in the mire of folly. 'Tis the crown and glory of organic sciences that it does thro' final cause, link material to moral;... You have ignored this link; and, if I do not mistake your meaning, you have done your best in one or two pregnant clauses to break it. Were it possible, which, thank God, it is not, to break it, humanity in my mind would suffer a damage that might brutalize it—and the human race into a lower grade of degradation than any into which it has fallen since its written record tells us of its history."[74]

The change in American culture since the 1947 Supreme Court decision in *Everson v. Board of Education,* teacher unionization, and tenure law has led to a colossal increase in family breakdown, abortion, homosexuality, use of addictive drugs, and burgeoning needs for hospital and prison space. Universities and colleges dominated by the old European secular philosophy have become havens for alcoholism and dorm cohabitation by unmarried students. Some state universities even have a department of religion dominated by atheists who serve as a campus mafia to destroy the academic standing of any faculty member who dares to suggest that there is such an alternative to Charles Darwin's *Origin of the Species* as intelligent design or a God of creation.

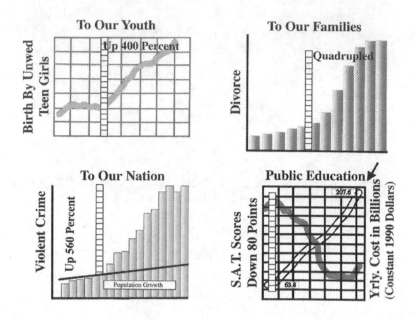

The ladder marks 1962 when the radical minority started to lever the God of creation and moral faith out of our schools.

The graphs reflect public reports up to 2009.

"The first national study of four common sexually transmitted diseases among girls and young women has found that one in four [is] infected with at least one of the diseases, US health officials reported Tuesday" (Lawrence K. Altman, The New York Times Tuesday, March 11, 2008). One in four US teenage girls have STDs. The diseases, which are infections caused by bacteria, viruses and parasites, can produce acute symptoms … and potentially fatal entopic pregnancy … and cervical cancer. The two most common sexually transmitted diseases, or STDs, among all the participants tested were HPV, at 18 percent, and Chlamydia, at 4 percent, according to the analysis, part of the National Health and Nutrition Examination Survey."[75]

"One of every 100 adults are in jail or prison, according to a new report documenting America's rank as the world's No. 1 incarcerator," according to a new study by the nonpartisan Pew Center on the States. With more than 2.3 million people behind bars, the United States leads the world in both the number and percentage of residents it incarcerates."[76]

These are merely symptoms of the consequences of the courts' detachment from government by written and permanent law. Far greater damage is the hidden loss to the soul of American youth.******

When collective bargaining unions had a monopoly for supplying railroad industry workers, the opportunity for truckers to compete by hauling freight gave the public an option and stopped costly exploitation by railroad employee unions. Employee unions dominated the auto industry, and cars were poorly made. It was competition from the manufacturers of foreign-made cars that restored quality to automobiles made by American auto manufacturers. And now it appears that at least two American auto manufacturers have been forced into bankruptcy or government takeover because of government-established unions that demand unreasonable wages for autoworkers. When Medieval European religious authoritarians achieved control of education in the Roman Catholic Church, it was competition sparked by the martyrs (the offended protesters were themselves Catholics) that brought about the great Reformation and gave the masses freedom from the despotic education monopoly.

Continued reliance on the promise of reforms made by government education professionals simply give tenured radicals more time to dumb down our most precious resource and engineer the "transformation of society."

****** Studies show that a significantly higher percentage of public schoolteachers send their children to private schools than non-teacher parents (George Archibald, The Washington Times, September 22, 2004, http://www.washingtontimes. com/news/2004/sep/22/20040922-122847-5968r/).

CHAPTER 10
Education That Is Profoundly American

Immigrants from diverse backgrounds came to America and worked peacefully together because they shared a common mind on the issue of human equality, moral law, and responsible citizenship. They wanted no more potentates, authoritarian clergy, professors, or kings. The *Constitution* clarified the point, when forbidding titles "of nobility," that could undermine the sovereign authority of the people under God over government (Section 9, article 8).

Children are not the property of the government or the state. The authority and responsibility for what children are taught rests with parents.

As shown in earlier chapters, the Founding Fathers recognized that the preservation of the family, self-government, and liberty depend upon applying the timeless and universal principles found in the Bible.. And for Americans to have firsthand knowledge of the Bible, they must be taught to read. Public school textbooks taught the alphabet through Bible verses that started with each letter. Abraham Lincoln's strong foundation in language was a result of his stepmother's curriculum—the Bible and Shakespeare (The Encyclopædia Britannica: a dictionary of arts, sciences …, Volume 16 By Hugh Chisholm, page 703).

Reliable education rests on respect for the First Principle, namely, the **God of Creation is man's benefactor**. Increases in knowledge are made possible by the connecting links of intelligible design. Irrefutable third-grade math, for instance, is a link to the latest advances in the physical sciences.

Albert Einstein and Bill Gates were university dropouts but not learning dropouts. They were challenged to learn about the unvarying reliability and order of creation's design.

The character-building curriculum now taught by homeschool parents and many Christian private schools is comparable to the curriculum taught in common schools and one-room neighborhood schools in early America. At that time, such schools often had, say, thirty students, some at nearly every grade level, with one teacher.

John Jay

John Jay is thought to be one of the most influential among the Founding Fathers. He served as president of the first Continental Congress and was the first chief justice of the United States. When Jay applied for admission to King's College in New York at the age of fourteen, one of the requirements he had to fulfill was to translate the first ten chapters of the Gospel of John from Greek into Latin."[77]

Abigail Adams

Abigail Adams, wife of John Adams, the second president of the United States, wrote to her young son, John Quincy, who would later become our sixth president: "Great learning and superior abilities, should you ever possess them, will be of little value and small Estimation, unless Virtue, Honor, Truth, and integrity are added to them. Adhere to those religious Sentiments and principles that were early installed into your mind and remember that you are accountable to your Maker for all your upon you to attend constantly and steadfastly to the precepts and instructions of your Father as you value the happiness of your Mother and your own welfare. His care and attention to you render many things unnecessary for me to write which I might otherwise do, but the inadvertency and Heedlessness of youth, requires line upon line and precept upon precept, and when enforced by the joint efforts of both parents will I hope have a due influence upon your Conduct, for dear as you are to me, I had much rather you should have found your Grave in the ocean you have crossed, or any untimely death crop you in your Infant years, rather than see you an immoral profligate or Graceless child."[78]

Noah Webster's textbooks, including the *Webster's Blue-Back Speller,* were standard for American schools until early 1930. Conversant in many languages, he spent several years writing the *Webster's Dictionary* that preceded the dictionary used in America today. His definitions were often supported by Scripture.

Webster taught school in West Hartford, Connecticut, and later served as a soldier during the American Revolution. He spent nine terms in the Connecticut legislature and three terms in the Massachusetts legislature. A strong proponent for convening the Constitutional Convention, he wrote what became Article I, Section 8 of the *Constitution.*

Webster was concerned that the youth of our nation would learn to check their emotions and avoid the fears and pitfalls of foolish imaginations. Karl Marx stirred up the emotions of heady intellectuals. With promises of a utopia, he captured millions who, to the great loss of their families and even nations, embraced secular popularism. The Webster dictionary defined emotions as the "strong impression, or vivid sensation that immediately produces a reaction. The nature of the reaction is to either 'appropriate and enjoy, or avoid and repel' the cause for the impression."[79]

The proposal for education advanced by Thomas Jefferson and James Madison and adopted by the University of Virginia provides an excellent formula for teaching American history and government. It provides indisputable evidence of the American principles that are imperative for education in the taxpayer-funded classroom.

The resolution stated that "all students shall be inculcated with the basic American principles of government ... None should be inculcated [taught] which are incompatible with those on which the Constitution of this State, and of the United States were genuinely based, in the common opinion." The resolution also stated that the faculty had a standard of responsibility and were required to teach affirmatively these unique American principles. Only after they had done so were they to teach the conflicting principles as such, judging them by the soundness of the American principles that served as a basis. The resolution then specified six writings that, in the board's opinion, reflected the unanimously supported principles unique to America that youth should be taught. "These documents were John Locke's *Essay Concerning the True Original Extent and End of Civil Government* (1690), Algernon Sidney's *Discourses Concerning Government* (1698), the *Declaration of Independence*, Washington's *Farewell Address*, the *Virginia Resolutions of 1799* (adopted by the Virginia legislature), and the *Federalist Papers*."[80]

A Well-Educated Student:
Speaks and writes accurately.
Listens attentively.
Is a reader.
Is honest at all times.
Is a person of prayer.
Has God-honoring goals.
Upholds the traditional family.

Is sensitive to the Word and to the will of God.

Is sensitive to the needs of others.

Handles success and defeat with grace.

Has convictions and stands for them.

Fulfills citizen duties to family, church, and country.

Is polite in his dealings with others.

Uses resources responsibly.

Recognizes the existence of absolute truth, which never
changes and applied serves as a very sure means for
personal development and success.

Uses gentle yet persuasive words, not physical
force, to communicate his position.

PART III:
Liberty and Responsibility

Chapters 11 and 12

O Then conquer we must, when our cause it is just, And this be our motto: "In God is our trust." And the star-spangled banner in triumph shall wave O'er the land of the free and the home of the brave! From the *"The Star-Spangled Banner"*

"The Star-Spangled Banner" was made the national anthem of the United States by a congressional resolution on March 3, 1931 (46 Stat. 1508, codified at 36 U.S.C. § 301), and signed by President Herbert Hoover.

Chapter 11
Appeasement Will Not Work

Citizen paralysis must end. When we observe secular militants without knowing their intentions, we arrive at faulty conclusions. Their determination is rooted in the fact that morality, the traditional family, and belief in God firmly undermine the power of hierarchical authoritarians. For them, deception in pursuit of their atheistic world is a virtue.

Robert Chandler, writes about David Horowitz's testimony before the Kansas House of Representatives regarding "academic freedom." Horowitz said: "Entire academic departments and fields are no longer devoted to scholarly pursuits, but have become ideological training and recruitment centers for radical causes." The departments most suspect are economics, health, history, English, political science, sociology, psychology, and anthropology. Add to these departments women's studies, queer studies, black liberation studies, Islamic studies, third-world studies, global warming studies, and so on—you get the picture (Robert Chandler, PhD, with experience in the Department of Defense, State, and the Central Intelligence Agency, *Shadow World*, One Massachusetts Ave., N.W. Washington, D.C., Regnery Publishing, 2008). David Horowitz writes later in his book *Radical Son,* New York: Free Press, 1997: "The Marxists and socialists who had been refuted by historical events were now the tenured establishment of the academic world. Marxism had produced the bloodiest and most oppressive regimes in human history." Citations are from the September 2010 *Journal* by Dr. David A. Noebel, published by Summit Ministries, Manitou Springs, CO.

Teachers do have rights, but ultimately they answer to those who pay their salaries. Teachers who cannot accept a contract with a school district that requires respect for the family and morality have but one alternative, which is to establish, fund, and teach in their private schools.

Appeasement will not work. There is no valid reason for the complaint of leftists that conservatives are one-sided and unreasonable in support of their basic principles. Secular militants do not compromise their atheistic dogma. The hope that they will change is foolish. To be at peace with their own belief in atheistic exclusivity, they must have control over and displace those who project higher standards. The struggle between the forces of liberty and those who want an atheistic-secular world is a war of wills. If we win, they will still be free to fund and promote their own schools. If they win, we will be slaves to Godless authoritarian rule.

By far the greatest peril to America today is internal. It is the secular militants' war against traditional American values. This started when taxpayer-funded universities foolishly caved in to the demand for the old European secular policy of unionization and teachers' independence (tenure guarantees). Now contemporary liberals gleefully impose their God-rejecting approach to life upon the minds of American youth in lower-level public schools.

Abraham Lincoln understood that it was the dangers from within America, *not* from the outside, that could destroy America. He stated: "What constitutes the bulwark of our own liberty and independence? It is not our frowning battlements, our bristling seacoasts, the guns of our war steamers, or the strength of our gallant and disciplined army. **Our defense is in the preservation of the spirit that prizes liberty as the heritage of all men, in all lands, everywhere. Destroy this spirit, and you have planted the seeds of despotism around your own doors.**"[81]

CHAPTER 12
Our Strategy for Victory:
Political Action—Citizen Power

Our duty as Americans is clear. Defending what is right is a cost of freedom that must be paid. It is the all-important principles advanced in the God-honoring *Declaration*, which provides the moral predicate essential to restrain the use of oppressive government. Had leaders and educators failed to convey, with boldness, the God-honoring principles from the beginning, America would be just another of the hapless nations that have flitted in and then out of history.

Under the providence of God, we have pushed back the frontiers of tyranny and evil time and again. America has freed more human beings from the clutches of evil than any nation on earth, and we are relatively only a young country. Even though continental Europe, in its posture of pseudo-sophistication, might consider us the country cousin in the family of nations, when those same Europeans needed to be rescued—often from themselves—we were there to rescue them. We have done it many times and in many ways, as we have around the world. At enormous cost to ourselves, we have gone into (and out of) dozens of nations in order to make the world a better place—even those nations that were our deadliest enemies, like Germany and Japan after World War II. What MacArthur did in Japan, and what the Marshall Plan accomplished in Europe, are without historical equal, and they indicate what we think our high calling on the planet really is (Dr. Jack Wheeler, *The Ugly Liberal American*, page 4, quoted by *The Schwarz Report*, May 2008, Volume 48, number 5).

Ernest Renan, the agnostic, warned his friends that were promoting a socialist utopia: "Let us enjoy the liberty of the sons of God, but let us take care lest we become accomplices in the diminution of virtue which would menace society if Christianity were to grow weak. What should we do without it? If Rationalism wishes to govern the world without regard to the religious needs of the soul, the experience of the French Revolution is there to teach us the consequences of such a blunder."[82]

The rudeness and even hatred exhibited by secular pathfinders when confronted with American principles gives politics a bad name. They cannot tell the truth and sell their leftist agenda. **This gives us a comparative advantage. Political involvement and persistence in broadcasting American values is a noble and necessary calling for every freedom-loving American.**

Strategic Priorities
Every Citizen Has the Power to Advance Liberty

1. Restoring educational traditions central to American greatness provides the very sure basis for strong families, prosperity, and limited government for, by, and of the people.

Liberty with prosperity came to America because the Founding Fathers had it right. They took self and all pretender gods off the throne, and they placed the King of Kings, the impartial, nonsectarian God of life and creation's nature, on the throne.

"Our fathers have earned and bought it for us, at the expense of their ease, their estates, their pleasure, and their blood. And liberty cannot be preserved without a general knowledge among the people, who have a right, from the frame of their nature, to knowledge, as their great Creator, who does nothing in vain, has given them understandings, and a desire to know; but besides this, they have a right, an indisputable, unalienable, indefeasible, divine right to that most dreaded and envied kind of knowledge, I mean, of the characters and conduct of their rulers. Rulers are no more than

attorneys, agents, and trustees for the people; and if the cause, the interest and trust, is insidiously betrayed, or wantonly trifled away, the people have a right to revoke the authority that they themselves have deputed, and to constitute abler and better agents, attorneys, and trustees. And the preservation of the means of knowledge among the lowest ranks, is of more importance to the public than all the property of all the rich men in the country" (John Adams, vice president under George Washington, and second president of the United States, *A Dissertation on the Canon and Feudal Law*, 1766 from *The Works of John Adams*, ... by his Grandson Charles F. Adams, Boston: Little, Brown and Co., 10 volumes).

We must broadcast anew and persist in upholding the **First Principle**, that it is **creation's God Who is man's Benefactor**. This is the basic principle upon which all other worthy principles follow. When the First Principle is *not* publicly upheld by educators (for students to learn), the standards of righteousness that are central to liberty and American greatness soon become fodder for distortion by atheistic secular militants.

When we as a people championed the spirit of the First Principle, **creation's God Who is man's Benefactor,** the meaning of *Declaration of Independence* was clear and the war of King George III and his army against Americans failed.

The reason many people are not joining in to oppose what is being done is that they have been kept in the dark about the God-rejecting worldview now being imposed upon captive student classrooms. Our duty now is to be very public about the fact that reliable standards for law come with knowledge of the **nonsectarian Creator-based meaning** of the *Declaration of Independence* and the First Amendment. In 1835 the significance of this connection was observed by the French lawyer, Alexis de Tocqueville, "... in America religion is the road to knowledge, and the observance of the divine laws leads man to civil freedom ... ."

In the American system of representative government, education central to American greatness will be restored if the people know how it has been altered. That is the purpose of this book. The author accepts no personal remuneration for his writing or service as President of Heartland Foundation, Inc. **If you have received important insights from this book, share it with people you know.** The documentation has been put in book form so that readers such as yourself can put it into the hands of as many people as you can.

"The only thing necessary for the triumph [of evil] is for good men to do nothing" (The Works of Edmund Burke in Nine Volumes, Vol. IX. ... 172)

2. **Parents, guardians, and grandparents who can afford it should support the enrollment of the children in God-honoring private schools or, if able, homeschool them. This is the most powerful political statement that Americans can make. That is the vanguard for a nationwide competitive school system enabling citizen choice.**

3. **Promote the election of candidates for public office who unabashedly oppose government tolerance for teacher union tenure laws.** Good teachers have always had tenure by virtue of the quality of their work.

"Because of the obvious potential for abuse even labor union advocates like AFL-CIO President George Meany and Franklin D. Roosevelt viewed unionization of the public employees as unthinkable."[83]

When tenure establishment privileges for government teachers are prohibited, good teachers can again safely support the traditional family and historic American principles without having their patriotism dirtied by secular gossips.

4. **Support legislative candidates who recognize the benefit of routing taxpayer revenues for education directly to parents or other guardians.** They may then choose homeschool, private school, or a charter school that reflects their values. Texas legislators are now even backing "charter colleges." They could be "core curriculum

charters" that would offer "great books seminars," including courses on the Bible, Renaissance, Reformation, and, of course, American values resident in the *Declaration of Independence.* Charter colleges would receive per-student funding as charter K–12 do now.[84]

5. **Elect people to serve on school boards who will insist that the unique and specific American principles for government be taught.** In 1877, the US government printing office published *The Organic Laws of the United States of America.* Ben Poole, who was then clerk of printing records, compiled the documentation under an order by the US Senate. *The Organic Laws of the United States of America* lists the *Declaration of Independence, Articles of Confederation, Northwest Ordinance,* and the *Constitution of the United States.* Share this study with your school board.

6. **Support candidates at federal and state levels who agree to work for the appointment of judges who respect the original meaning of the *Constitution.***

"Judge Robert H. Bork describes the enormous damage that activist judges have inflicted on America in his book, *Coercing Virtue: The Worldwide Rule of Judges.* The courts are often dominated by faux intellectuals of the Left who, unable to persuade the people or the legislators, 'avoid the verdict of the ballot box' by engaging in 'politics masquerading as law.' We are 'increasingly governed not by law or elected representatives, but by unelected, unrepresentative, unaccountable committees of lawyers applying no law other than their own will.'"[85]

7. **Work for and elect senators and representatives to the U.S. Congress who will reassert their duty to represent the people and restore the Constitutional provisions for restricting the role of federal judges.**

The *Constitution* is a rule of law document, not a rule by unelected judges. In terms of how authority manifests itself over time, the two contrasts represent the distinction between representative government of, by, and for the people and the tyranny of authoritarianism. In terms of philosophy, the two represent the distinction between the Creator-based *Declaration of Independence* and the evils of old European secular philosophy. When the traditional American sovereignty of man under God over government was adopted on July 4, 1776, it reversed the historical inevitability of authoritarian carnage.

The *Declaration,* unanimously adopted by Congress, made four specific references to political reliance upon Higher Authority. This was not done hesitatingly.*******
—Higher authority is the resource that feeds the branches of liberty, "the laws of Nature and Nature's God "
—"That all men are created equal, that they are endowed by their Creator with certain unalienable rights …"
—"Appealing to the Supreme Judge of the world for the rectitude of our intentions …"
—"With a firm reliance on the protection of divine Providence …"

A liberal judge says we do make mistakes. What we are talking about is not mere mistakes. Liberty-loving Americans need to be blunt about this. What we are talking about is the colossal error of rejecting the universal and impartial laws of nature and creation's God that reversed thousands of years of authoritarian exploitation and human deprivation. We have a National Day of Prayer. We have paid chaplains in our Congress and military to emphasize the importance of religious faith. When the Supreme Court comes out, the crier yells, "God save America." This was made even more explicit when in 1954, "One nation under God" was added for the invocation of the Pledge of Allegiance. It is time to expose the fascistic exclusivity of the pagan religion demanded by liberal-minded judges, educators, and politicians.

Congress has limited the courts several times in the past. By the authority of Article I, Section 8, of the *Constitution,* the representatives we elect to Congress "shall have power … to constitute tribunals inferior to the

---

******* For a review of the harmful laws imposed by unelected judges, see Chapter 6 in this book and "High Courts and Misdemeanors" by R. P. George, at http://touchstonemag.com/archives/print.php?id=17-08-026-f.

Supreme Court." Article III, Section 1, reads: "The judicial power of the United States, shall be vested in one Supreme Court, and in such inferior courts as the Congress may from time to time ordain and establish." Article III, Section 2, reads: "The Supreme Court shall have appellate jurisdiction, both as to law and fact, with **such exceptions**, and under the regulations as the Congress shall make."

Looking to the future, at such time as the American people elect Senators and Representatives who are committed to reining in supremacist judges, a plan for **"such exceptions,"** provided for by Article III, Section 2, should be at hand. These exceptions would also be the talking points until the corrective change is achieved.

The following **exception** would be effective: Any future court decisions that reflect upon the first ten amendments that are not clearly linked to their meaning, as understood, prior to 1947 would be classified as a **Supreme Court Interim Opinion** or some similar designation. Going back to 1947 is a heavy lift, but it only applies to future court decisions that hinge upon the so foundational basis for "government of laws, and not of men." Categories of law that are not related to the first ten amendments would be exempt from the Supreme Court Interim Opinion requirement. If the legislative branch does not pass laws to solve the problem dealt within a **Supreme Court Interim Opinion** within a specified period of time (for example, three years), the court decision would expire regardless of the ramifications.

Adoption of the **Supreme Court Interim Opinion** requirement by Congress blends with the legislative and judicial separation of powers without undermining judicial independence, and it is consistent with the constitutional system of checks and balances. Our representatives in Congress would then bear responsibility for treatment of the problem, and the Supreme Court would be shielded from the bleeding of reprehensible engineering imposed by unelected judges.

Going back to the 1947 precedent requirement is a logical time for **instituting the Interim Opinion** requirement. It was in 1947 that the

Supreme Court majority twisted and undermined the citizens' First Amendment protections from government-established authoritarians.

Stare decisis is no excuse for preserving bad court precedents. *Stare decisis* is legal talk for an everyday practice that we all follow. It simply means that once a decision is implemented, it should be supported for a considerable period of time to see if, in fact, it is helping or, at a minimum, not doing harm. When a law is proven to be harmful, that law should be reversed. The practice of preserving court precedent was never intended to be a mandate for national suicide.

8. This suggestion is for our friends in the Judiciary. If there is a better approach than instituting a **Supreme Court Interim Opinion** requirement for restoring sanity to the judiciary, then have that approach be the public goal. Determining a better approach is the duty of conservative lawyers and judges, who are better situated to frame a solution. The recommendation needs to be reasonable and would require an ongoing, nationwide sales campaign until it is successful. This would best be determined by a citizen Congress composed of conservative lawyers, law professors, and judges, convened to make recommendations for restoring the rule of law. The Congress should involve participants from every state, be privately funded, and meet in secret for the same reasons the Constitutional Convention met in secret. This Congress would compare in importance to the decision-making phase for the judiciary conducted by the Constitutional Convention.

The most important of all the amendments is the First Amendment. This is demonstrably true. It was not until secular militants were leveraged by the 1947 Supreme Court's *Everson v. Board of Education* decision that the role of moral absolutes ceased to be standard in government schools. For 190 years the Judeo-Christian basis for citizen self-rule was vigorously taught. Non-denominational prayers and the Pledge of Allegiance were practiced in classrooms. For several decades now the moral religions, most directly Christianity, have been under systematic attack by liberal judges. Americans can agree with the following quote as long as any conflict between amendments to the Constitution are

126

reconciled by having the First Amendment, in its original meaning up until 1947, held supreme. "A constitution, like any other document, is to be read as a whole. The court, in the language of the lawyers, 'will take the instrument by its four corners' and read each part in the light of the rest. Since written constitutions come into effect through popular assent, the meaning intended by the people would be sought by the courts. The common understanding of the words at the time the language was employed is therefore of cogent significance. This consideration, however, will not prevent the application of the terms employed to conditions arising later and not contemplated at the time the language was adopted.... There is an ancient rule of statutory construction, coming down through Blackstone, that in seeking the true meaning of legislative language the court will take cognizance of the 'old law, the mischief and the remedy.' The rule is useful in constitutional construction."[86]

9. **It is important that we reassess how our personal giving and tax dollars are being used.** Of utmost importance, we need to oppose funding any higher or lower public school that places in question the primacy of the traditional family, morality, and citizen self-reliance. The following letter is an example of sorely needed citizen influence.

Dear County Treasurer:

We are paying the education tax called for by the billing from your office. This is, of course, an important citizen duty. We respectfully urge that legislators change the tax law so collections for school tuition would be routed to the parents or guardians, who can then exercise their right to choose a school, be it public or private, that best represents and teaches their values. There are many ways to administer this, including the very effective tuition program known as the G.I. Bill. We agree with parents and many teachers who object to any curriculum forced upon students that places the composition of the family in question and presents revisionist morality as an acceptable lifestyle.

Thank you for your work as County Treasurer.

(Signed) _____

10. Prayer, humility, and recommitment must be undertaken. The selfless dedication that made the American Revolution possible is seen in the great awakening of 1740 through 1780. God has provided this specific promise: "If my people, which are called by my name, shall humble themselves, and pray, and seek my face, and turn from their wicked ways; then will I hear from heaven, and will forgive their sin, and will heal their land" (2 Chron. 7:14).

PART IV:
Supplemental Material

Appendix A through E

APPENDIX A
Grand Jury Presentment
Problems in Higher Education

It was my privilege to chair a Grand Jury for the Eleventh Judicial District of Iowa that investigated activities at Iowa State University and made several recommendations for changes in higher education.

This study of higher education is even more relevant now than when adopted December 23, 1968. With the imposition of teacher unions and tenure laws, radicals in the soft sciences now dominate lower-level public education.

News reports had made it clear that drugs, immorality, and disrespect for constitutional authority had become an ongoing part of the academic menu in our universities. With about six months left in our term, I suggested to the county attorney, Charles Vanderbur, that the jury investigate what was going on at Iowa State University. He said, "Dave, I'll do anything I can to help you." He provided us with tape recordings of campus presentations by radicals. After hearing the first tape, the jury members gave the go-ahead to undertake an investigation. The jury's chief concern was the education environment and its impact upon the behavioral patterns and decision-making ability of students.

My challenge as the foreman was to obtain unanimous agreement for significant recommendations from three Republican and three Democrat jurors. Several legislative directives for changes in the administration of Iowa's colleges and universities followed the release of the study.

Because of tenured radicals embedded in the system, the impact of the Presentment faded within four or five years. The Grand Jury report received nationwide media attention, and requests for copies of the Presentment came from government officials in Iowa, California, and Washington, DC.

"As one of the tens of thousands who admire the action of your Grand Jury, I wish to commend Foreman Norris and his jury for their courageous and true Americanism in focusing public attention on the perverted minority ... who would destroy what we have ... in America and deliver us unto our enemies." (E. Allen, Burlington, North Dakota, letter to the Nevada, Iowa *Journal*)

"OUT IN IOWA ... The jury's report said 'there is a need for increased emphasis at all levels of education of the American ideal. Our soldiers have been dying for this ideal. Education as never before should clearly teach it.' So say we." (from the *Boston Record*, printed in the *Ames Daily Tribune*)

Ames, Iowa–(AP)–The Grand Jury wants "moral pollution" ... "and defamation of our country" (in the Humanities curriculum) stopped. (*Denver Post*)

With a prestigious media network, political, religious, and social studies courses, statewide extension offices, and an adult education outreach, universities possessed (and still possess) immense power to shape public opinion. The president of the university and campus radicals did everything they could to discredit the Grand Jury's work. Initially, however, news of the Presentment was unimpeded. The university president and all members of the Iowa Board of Regents except one were out of the state during Christmas break when the Presentment became public.

Except for the coverage in the *Des Moines Register* and a few radical student publications, most news reports were accurate. Those who were critical were very spirited in their objections. A January 8, 1969, *Des*

Moines Register headline read, "ISU President Lashes Out at 'Distorted' Report by Jury." Later, the Iowa State University Press published a book for the Iowa Civil Liberties Union entitled *Freedom in Iowa*. This publication showered ISU President Robert Parks and the liberal presidents of the other two universities in Iowa with honors and attacked the work and reputation of several Iowa leaders, past and present, including myself.

I was later told that an Iowa State University administrative vice president was briefing the incoming extension course attendees and denigrating the work of the jury. Eventually, a county extension officer attending one of the on-campus short courses stood up and strongly criticized the vice president's presentation, and his practice of criticizing the jury report ended.

The Grand Jury Presentment itself was well documented. One news article reported that the Iowa Civil Liberties Union had decided they would not sue the Grand Jury. Another paper reported that an ongoing effort had failed to get the new judge, Harvey Uhlenhopp, serving the Eleventh Judicial District to dismiss the Presentment. Within two years, Judge Uhlenhopp was elevated to the Iowa Supreme Court.

I was concerned that some reporters and editors would misrepresent the Grand Jury Presentment. Consequently, reporters were told that I would respond to inquiries in writing only, and this brought their interest to a halt. I personally received approximately a hundred letters from citizens, all of whom praised the jury's work.

Arrangements were made for a local print shop to reproduce and handle requests for copies of the Presentment. Later, I received a call from them informing me that the university had purchased the remaining copies, so I instructed them to print five hundred more.

The Grand Jury members all contributed to the report. There was a considerable amount of material to review. A few campus administrators and members of the faculty met with us to give their perspective. Following each meeting, I wrote a brief of what seemed relevant and presented it to the jury members at the next meeting. The members approved most of my draft, which later became the Presentment, unanimously approved by the jury.

Portions of the Presentment follow, with words added for clarification in parentheses. Supplemental ideas are enclosed in boxes.

Grand Jury Presentment *Problems in Higher Education*

Power to Capture a Nation
Through Indoctrination of Its Youth

For many years, psychologists and educators have recognized the processes by which thought and behavioral patterns acquired in youth become the basis for adult motivation. In modern times, thoughtful observers have become progressively aware that moral, social, and political concepts implanted during the time of mental immaturity not only participate in the conduct later in life, but, once acquired, become dominant and often unalterable in the adult. Thus, captive audiences of immature minds provide powerful and much prized forums for anti-Judeo-Christian, anti-American indoctrination.

Educational environments, left unguarded [by politically active citizens and wise legislators], can easily be captured by alien militants and, in due course, transformed into climates of unquestioned social and political opinion.

Dr. I. L. Kandell, a refugee from Romania and professor at Columbia University, aptly lamented education devoid of established knowledge, calling it "the most Communist feature of the Communist Revolution and the most Nazi expression of the National Socialist Revolution."

A modern term for the atheistic-secular worldview is "political correctness." Opposing points of view, namely morality, religious liberty, traditional marriage, and the political principles upon which America has prospered, are censored from textbooks and teacher presentations.

The American Ideal Reflected in
the Constitutions of the States

> Control over the use of government power has always been a test of wills. The Judeo-Christian approach to government was vehemently opposed by atheists during the writing of the Iowa Constitution. The following quotations are from the *Constitution of the State of Iowa*, which is similar to many other state constitutions.

1. Preamble: "We, the People of the State of Iowa, grateful to the Supreme Being for the blessings hitherto enjoyed, and feeling our dependence on Him for a continuation of those blessings, do ordain and establish a free and independent government, by the name of the STATE OF IOWA."

2. Article I, Section 2: "Government is instituted (by the people) for the protection, security and benefit of the people."

3. Article I, Section 1: "All men are, by nature, free and equal, and have certain inalienable rights—among which are those of enjoying and defending life and liberty, acquiring, possessing and protecting property, and pursuing and obtaining safety and happiness."

4. Article I, Section 2: "All political power is inherent in the people."

5. Article I, Section 2: "They (the people) have the right at all times, to alter or reform the government, whenever the public good may require it."

6. Provision for unrestricted exchange of ideas for education and government policy, no matter how radical, is provided through frequent elections: candidates for office must go before the public and be chosen by mature citizens at the ballot box.

7. Article IX, Section 3: "The General Assembly shall encourage by all suitable means the *intellectual, scientific, moral and agricultural improvement.*"

Observations in the Problem Area

Following the publication of the Grand Jury Presentment, the Iowa State University Press published a book for the Iowa Civil Liberties Union entitled *Freedom in Iowa*. Among many false statements in the book was the claim that the Grand Jury "never defined" the word *radicals*. The Grand Jury's description of radicals follows.

At this point perhaps we should define to some extent what we mean in this report by "radicals" and "militants" in the context of their behavior on campus (and) as expressed in our interviews and investigation.

I. Their number one goal, both stated and apparent, is that they desire to control the useful university apparatus for a base to promote and direct their activities. There is no apparent limit; [they want to control the] university news media, selection of guest speakers, extension outlets, *et cetera*.

An example of the power of radicals at ISU was brought to our attention by a citizen who had contacted a department head. He suggested that the coming News Editors' Seminar might be informed by the University of an Official Pamphlet about the techniques of Communist propaganda in the news media. The citizen was told that it was not the business of the university to get involved in politics. The citizen was later shocked to read in the newspaper that an associate professor of history had lectured the editors on possible future problems with certain [conservative] local political groups.

This News Editors' Seminar provided by the university was clearly a political program intended to undermine the rights, credibility, and opinions of citizens who oppose leftist agendas for government and radicals' control of the soft sciences in taxpayer-funded education.

II. They have a general goal of destroying and tearing down traditional values. [Hateful talk leads to hateful acts, and immoral advocacy leads to immoral acts.] Radical salesmen appeal to idealistic students with words calculated to destroy their youthful faith in their heritage. The following quotations [provided by the County Attorney to the jury] are from one of many paid speakers at ISU.

"I spend about 90 percent of my time now on college campuses. This is the most morally polluted, insane nation on the face of this earth and it is your job to change it."

"And I say to you youngsters in the process of trying to make this peacefully orderly transition of bringing up the constitution over the capitalists, if they offer you too much resistance, then destroy them."

"Let's always remember that flag still ain't nothing but a rag, like all of the other flags on the face of this earth."

This was not an isolated example but [was] typical of much of the educational approach we observed.

In the area of society and human nature, such denial, when implemented, detaches future generations from past experience. Oddly enough, that is the very reason taxpayers fund colleges and universities. Tolerating such foolishness gives a teaching license to those who promote illicit sex, the use of decimating drugs, flag burning, and other immoral behavior [that questions] historically known good.

Such a position on fundamental tenets raises a very interesting question. If the desirability of sexual virtue and the undesirability of co-habitation in single student dorms is, as they say, a matter of opinion—if in fact sexual virtue and many other tenets such as basic honesty are not established knowledge suitable for classroom doctrine—what is the good of having humanities [soft science behavioral studies] courses at all? When a radical teacher lectures, what is he accomplishing with taxpayers' money?

III. Radicals use tactics that blatantly ignore the basic teaching standard of honesty. It is not unusual to hear them proclaim the virtues of equality and love, and extol violence, hatred and the use of harmful drugs in the same speech. In their effort to present a one-sided picture, they suppress opposing views. One jury interviewee [a professor] stated his concern—if students hear a lie often enough, some will believe it!

IV. Radicals' tactics are aggressive, domineering and, when needed, ruthless in character. In such cases, students and other teachers with average courtesy are no match. The most aggressive [teachers] prevail over those who feel obligated to spend their time teaching and learning rather than contending with and being buffeted by verbal terrorism. One of the radicals' tactics is rule by policy committee domination. They pressure administrators to relinquish their duty in a specific area and turn it over to a committee.

These practices by employees all fall below what the taxpaying public, in our opinion, expect and have a right to expect of the teachers they hire.

Summary

The concrete evidence of failures is well illustrated by the article entitled "New Left's Boasts: We Are Organizing Sedition." According to the article, the *New York Times* asked an Iowa State University student where he picked up his radical ideas. The student referred to a teacher by name and concluded, "He was a history teacher here (Iowa State University) two years ago. I took a course in *Ideas of Western Civilization* from him. That got me started." There is no doubt that some teachers are guilty of using their status to effectively subvert or undermine the morals and allegiance of some students.

> Friedrich A. Hayek said, regarding sectarian missionaries, "The whole intellectual climate [is a] complete perversion of language.... Collectivism means the end of truth ... The most effective way of making people accept the validity of the values they are to serve is to persuade them that they are really the same as those which they, or at least the best among them, have always held, but which were not properly understood or recognized before" (Friedrich A. Hayek, *The Road to Serfdom*, Britain, Rutledge, 1944, 174).

The atheistic humanist approach to education is illustrated by events at ISU. Using scurrilous charges, tenured academic mafia undermined academic freedom and forced the discontinuation of a very popular university course dealing with creation science. The course violated the secular dogma upon which their God-rejecting theory of evolution, anti-Americanism, and anti-morality are constructed. The course, taught by a highly ranked professor administrator at Iowa State University, was discontinued, and the professors who bullied that decision into effect did not receive so much as a reprimand.

According to an article in the *Ames Tribune,* May 12, 2007, "Guillermo Gonzalez … [was] denied tenure this semester by Iowa State University." In this event that became known to the public, Iowa State University denied tenure to gifted astronomer Guillermo Gonzalez, who made the mistake of writing a book that included academic support for intelligent design. At the same time, the university promoted to full professor with tenure rights in the soft sciences an outspoken leftist, Hector Avalos. As a religious studies professor, he served as the adviser to the ISU Atheist Society.

Our investigation indicates that the main reason for the youthful rebellion and attitude of carelessness in student morals is their loss of confidence in the wisdom embedded in their heritage. Failure to clearly implant these truths detaches future generations from past experience, the very basis of education.

In the field of morality, all basic truths have been apprehended. All the changing conditions we hear so much about do not affect the validity or applicability of the central directives of human conduct. These truths are demonstrated both by their benefits and by the consequences of disregarding them—those who do fall easily into lawlessness, and harmful addictions, *et cetera*. **There is no greater contribution a teaching institution can make to human progress and purpose than to endow students at all levels with this knowledge.**

Those who place their present faith and future hope in law enforcement to conduct humanity to brighter times ignore a fundamental psychological truth. Legal and material attempts to correct human conduct resulting from improper training must all end in failure. It is impossible to superimpose an effective code of ethics through compulsion. Police force provides nothing more corrective than temporary control of faulty behavior that is traceable to education's failure to implant established knowledge of morality and the precepts of individual responsibility.

Where to Go for the Solution

The frustrating inability of the public to correct the distortion of academic freedom is due, in the Grand Jury's view, to the failure of the people to see the continuation of the atrocious abuses by radicals as the breakdown in the responsibility-authority-control principle that it really is. Any organization, educational or otherwise, is an attempt at cooperation. Cooperation is not possible unless responsibility and authority go hand-in-hand.

The parents and taxpayers delegated a portion of their responsibility and authority, through an administrative chain-of-command, for the selection of educators who want to teach and [who] agree with public policy.

The system of organization varies in the several states, but in Iowa the Board of Regents (chosen by the Governor) is responsible to the public for education at the state universities. It is … the Board of Regents who must lay down corrective policy on behalf of the people. If the problem is not corrected … the public must impose changes as necessary.

The taxpayers, having the final responsibility for the universities, quite properly should have the authority to change the Board of Regents' membership or take other measures if they find themselves in disagreement with Board policy. If the established procedures for governing at this level leave the Regents insensitive to public interest, then it is time to update governing procedures.

The citizen public, having given the Board of Regents [in this case] the responsibility to implement public policy, must also leave them the authority to go to the university president, who has the executive responsibility of the university. The university president, vested with the responsibility by the Board of Regents, has the authority to [replace] his aides if he believes they are not carrying out his ideas [in the public interest].

Most Important Educational Change Needed

1. Regents' policy changes which will sufficiently define and implement the elimination of moral pollution by faculty and paid speakers will by all suitable means encourage "moral ... improvement" (*Constitution of the State of Iowa, Article IX, 2nd School ... Sec. 3*).

2. There is a need for increased emphasis on the American ideal at all levels of education. We believe this ideal needs to be a continuing emphasis from kindergarten through maturity. Our revolutionary concepts are a most exciting and important subject.

It seems rather clear that the nerve center for society, the power for social revolution, is inherent in the adult electorate rather than in the schools, and that the radical missionaries should be sent to the electorate, not to the captive audience of youthful minds.

The idea ... that the people of this land should not be trusted with the complexities of education is absurd. The greatness of America places the educational and political emphasis under the control of the people. This approach is much safer than providing a haven [tenure guarantees] for ... teachers.

Our soldiers have been dying for this ideal. Education, as never before, should clearly teach it. Even in imperfection, it has achieved greatness for Americans unparalleled in history. Every individual is important, and the mature public make the decisions over government—something that atheistic, humanist-based governments do not and cannot provide.

Right of Taxpayers to Control Education Challenged

Who has academic freedom, the parent/taxpayer or the teacher? Is the parent, who once had academic freedom, now to be deprived because a teacher was hired? Most agree that anyone can teach what he pleases on his own, but must not [take advantage of his own] academic freedom by robbing taxpayers of their freedom to direct public education in the public's interest, based upon the learning process and established knowledge.

Problems Compound If Not Corrected

No single level of education should be considered in a vacuum.... But it is going on! The students of colleges are, after all, the graduates of American elementary and secondary schools. We, the adults and teachers of today, are the graduates of high schools, colleges, and universities in the recent past. Not only are various levels of American education interrelated, but the problems also feed back upon one another to produce a complex of relationships that affect us all and must be handled wisely. In professions such as medicine or architecture, failures soon become apparent and are corrected. A faulty experiment impacting the socio/political mindset may not be detected for two or three generations, when it is too late to reverse and avoid disaster.

—End of Presentment—

The purpose of universities was freedom for competition of ideas in search of truth. What has happened is the advocates of atheistic-secular totalitarianism applied their art and removed competition from the soft sciences. When citizen control of universities, colleges, and now virtually all lower-level public schools was hijacked by faculty independence (teachers union mechanization and teacher tenure guarantees), tyranny was bound to follow. What we now have is tyranny against the moral fiber of our youth and nation. This is the inevitable result of [imposing] "German graduate methods [faculty independence] onto American campuses in the late nineteenth century ... academic freedom became a cause celebre."

At the time of the Grand Jury study, we did not realize the linkage between the American Association of University Professors (AAUP) and what appears to be their prosecution arm, the leftist American Civil Liberties Union (ACLU). The book *Freedom in Iowa*, published by the Iowa State University Press, promoted the Iowa Civil Liberties Union, bringing this connection to my attention.

Teacher employee contracts, structured according to ACLU definitions for academic freedom and tenure, shift the decision-making authority for removing radical teachers away from the president of the university, who is hired by the public to superintend the institution. It is now the aggressive tenured faculty, not the president, who have control over who teaches and what is taught. Instead of being an administrator, the university president works full-time quieting campus disputes, promoting campus expansion, and raising money by lobbying alumni and legislators. Sensing this kind of environment, the US Supreme Court held in a dispute that professors at Yeshiva University in New York City were managerial [administrators], not employees within the meaning of the National Labor Relations Act, and hence the university administrators were not required to bargain with the union that represented the professors. The Court noted: "Budget requests prepared by the senior professor in each subject area receive the 'perfunctory' approval of the Dean '99 percent' of the time and have never been rejected by the central administration. The faculty ... effectively determine curriculum, grading systems ... matriculation standards" (*NLRB v. Yeshiva University*, 582 F.2d 686, 1978, *affd* 444 US 672, 1980).

The ACLU/AAUP version of academic freedom and tenure that enables radicals to reject the public standards for what is taught and not taught is not a legal concept. Without the control of the citizens who established the schools and pay the bills, what is taught is wholly dependent upon the internal culture of the faculty at the universities and the government grade schools. This problem is systemic.

"The *1940 Statement of Principles on Academic Freedom and Tenure* by the American Association of University Professors has no legal effect, but the AAUP publicly censures colleges and universities that they believe have violated [their version of] academic freedom. However, nearly all [not all] of the colleges and universities have adopted this statement or a variation of the statement which is contained in the faculty policy manual of each college or university, and it is incorporated by reference in the employment contract between the university and each individual faculty member" (Dr. Ronald B. Standler, "Academic Freedom in the USA," http://www.rbs2.com/afree.htm).

The penetrating damage imposed because of tenure laws sheltering radical professors and teachers in the soft sciences must be [reversed]. The authority of taxpayer/parents to control what is taught in government institutions must be restored. By routing education revenues directly to the parents or guardians, sanity will be restored to education. The many thousands of honest and morally upright teachers will again have the unimpeded support of the citizen consensus. Not only will what is taught be cleaned up, but also competition between education suppliers will reduce the cost [and increase the quality] of public education.

The voice in the chorus of concerned citizens is imperative. What confronts the American family and voter electorate is a test of wills. School administrators must be able to fire leftist teachers [without spending] years and … tens of thousands of taxpayers' dollars defending education from the [resulting] lawsuits imposed by ACLU lawyers and the imperial arm of radical judges. To effect change, active citizen involvement in the political process must exceed the determination of those who are using political circumvention to destroy the family and liberty.

GRAND JURY REPORT

Moral Faults at Iowa State Hit

By CELIENE NOLD BRUCE

AMES, Iowa—(AP)—A grand jury in Story County, Iowa, wants "moral pollution by faculty and paid "speakers" at Iowa State University discouraged by changes in the humanities curriculum.

"The militant, radical activist, both teacher and student, is involved in the humanities," said the jury after a three-month investigation.

UP TO BOARD

The jury said it was up to the State Board of Regents to make "corrective" policy changes, and said regents' membership should be changed if the public isn't satisfied with what it does.

"There is a need for increased emphasis at all levels of education of the American ideal," the jury report said. "Our soldier boys have been dying for this ideal. Education as never before should clearly teach it."

The jury said it began the investigation after frequent reports of "student radicals and other activists using campus media to pulpiteer, sensational-

DENVER POST

12/29/68

ize and otherwise promote illicit sex, drug use, draft evasion, and defamation of our country."

ISU, around state the nin "Is the Bo definiti sibility discont liars, our he ples or ic free The that ha the hu lem "p admini "level The who tr "faith nothin their o "Our by the about are in much have jority world, "Wh tures, with What ward moral

---

January 21, 1969 *Page 1*

LETTERS TO THE EDITOR

January 15, 1969

Editor, The Journal:

As one of the tens of thousands who admire the action of your Grand Jury, I wish to commend Foreman Norris and his jury for their courageous and true Americanism, in focusing Public attention on the perverted minority anarchists who would destroy what we have left in American, and deliver us unto our enemies.

As one who has always been proud of ISU, let me express my shame for its leaders who were not wise enough to remain quiet — evidence of the apparent determination of High Education to continue its sucidial plunge of self destruction. And believe me, few of your readers have spent more time or money on Education than I.

Patriotic Americans are demanding that funds to these perverted elements be CUT OFF! This is the one language the anarchists and their teachers understand.

Very truly yours,
E. Allen
Box 502
Burlington, N.D.

Nevada Journal Tuesday

Out in Iowa

From the Boston Record, edition of Jan. 7, 1969:

"They don't kid around out in Iowa. A grand jury there wants 'moral pollution by faculty and paid speakers' at Iowa State University discouraged by changes in the humanities curriculum. The grand jury charged that 'the militant radical activist, both teacher and-student, is involved in the humanities,' and called on the State Board of Regents to make 'corrective' policy changes.

"The jury began the investigation after reports of 'student radicals and other activists using campus media to pulpiteer, sensationalize and otherwise promote illicit sex, drug use, draft evasion, and defamation of our country.'

"The jury's report said 'there is a need for increased emphasis at all levels of education of the American ideal. Our soldiers have been dying for this ideal. Education as never before should clearly teach it.' So say we."

Ames Daily **Tribune**
Tues., Jan. 14, 1969

APPENDIX B
State of Iowa Bill of Rights

This law follows the right to life and to liberty from government oppression, principles of the *Declaration of Independence.*

Protection of the citizens from authoritarian judges depends upon preserving the intent of the law in the matter of unalienable citizen rights. This depends upon discontinuation of fascistic tenure guarantees that empower leftist law professors to prevent the school administrators from controlling what is taught to those who may later become judges.

Preamble. WE THE PEOPLE OF THE STATE OF IOWA, grateful to the Supreme Being for the blessings hitherto enjoyed, and feeling our dependence on Him for a continuation of those blessings, do ordain and establish a free and independent government, by the name of the State of Iowa, the boundaries whereof shall be as follows:

ARTICLE I. BILL OF RIGHTS.
Rights of persons. SECTION 1. All men and women are, by nature, free and equal, and have certain inalienable rights—among which are those of enjoying and defending life and liberty, acquiring, possessing and protecting property, and pursuing and obtaining safety and happiness. Amended 1998, Amendment [45]
Political power. SEC. 2. All political power is inherent in the people. Government is instituted for the protection, security, and benefit of the

people, and they have the right, at all times, to alter or reform the same, whenever the public good may require it.

Religion. SEC. 3. The general assembly shall make no law respecting an establishment of religion, or prohibiting the free exercise thereof; nor shall any person be compelled to attend any place of worship, pay tithes, taxes, or other rates for building or repairing places of worship, or the maintenance of any minister, or ministry.

Religious test—witnesses. SEC. 4. No religious test shall be required as a qualification for any office, or public trust, and no person shall be deprived of any of his rights, privileges, or capacities, or disqualified from the performance of any of his public or private duties, or rendered incompetent to give evidence in any court of law or equity, in consequence of his opinions on the subject of religion; and any party to any judicial proceeding shall have the right to use as a witness, or take the testimony of, any other person not disqualified on account of interest, who may be cognizant of any fact material to the case; and parties to suits may be witnesses, as provided by law. Referred to in §729.1 of the Code

Dueling. SEC. 5. Repealed 1992, Amendment [43]

Laws uniform. SEC. 6. All laws of a general nature shall have a uniform operation; the general assembly shall not grant to any citizen, or class of citizens, privileges or immunities, which, upon the same terms shall not equally belong to all citizens.

Liberty of speech and press. SEC. 7. Every person may speak, write, and publish his sentiments on all subjects, being responsible for the abuse of that right. No law shall be passed to restrain or abridge the liberty of speech, or of the press. In all prosecutions or indictments for libel, the truth may be given in evidence to the jury, and if it appears to the jury that the matter charged as libellous was true, and was published with good motives and for justifiable ends, the party shall be acquitted.

Personal security—searches and seizures. SEC. 8. The right of the people to be secure in their persons, houses, papers and effects, against unreasonable seizures and searches shall not be violated; and no warrant shall issue but on probable cause, supported by oath or affirmation, particularly describing the place to be searched, and the persons and things to be seized.

Right of trial by jury—due process of law. SEC. 9. The right of trial by jury shall remain inviolate; but the general assembly may authorize trial by a jury of a less number than twelve men in inferior courts; but no person shall be deprived of life, liberty, or property, without due process of law. See also R.Cr.P. 2.17, 2.21(2), 2.67; R.C.P. 1.902, 1.903, 1.1108

Rights of persons accused. SEC. 10. In all criminal prosecutions, and in cases involving the life, or liberty of an individual the accused shall have a right to a speedy and public trial by an impartial jury; to be informed of the accusation against him, to have a copy of the same when demanded; to be confronted with the witnesses against him; to have compulsory process for his witnesses; and, to have the assistance of counsel. See §602.1601 of the Code

When indictment necessary—grand jury. SEC. 11. All offenses less than felony and in which the maximum permissible imprisonment does not exceed thirty days shall be tried summarily before an officer authorized by law, on information under oath, without indictment, or the intervention of a grand jury, saving to the defendant the right of appeal; and no person shall be held to answer for any higher criminal offense, unless on presentment or indictment by a grand jury, except in cases arising in the army, or navy, or in the militia, when in actual service, in time of war or public danger.

The grand jury may consist of any number of members not less than five, nor more than fifteen, as the general assembly may by law provide, or the general assembly may provide for holding persons to answer for any criminal offense without the intervention of a grand jury. Paragraph 2 added 1884, Amendment [9]; Paragraph 1 amended 1998, Amendment [46]; As to indictment and the number of grand jurors, see R.Cr.P. 2.3, 2.4; Magistrate jurisdiction, see §602.6405 of the Code

Twice tried—bail. SEC. 12. No person shall after acquittal, be tried for the same offence. All persons shall, before conviction, be bailable, by sufficient sureties, except for capital offences where the proof is evident, or the presumption great.

Habeas corpus. SEC. 13. The writ of habeas corpus shall not be suspended, or refused when application is made as required by law, unless in case of rebellion, or invasion the public safety may require it.

Military. SEC. 14. The military shall be subordinate to the civil power. No standing army shall be kept up by the state in time of peace; and in time of war, no appropriation for a standing army shall be for a longer time than two years.

Quartering soldiers. SEC. 15. No soldier shall, in time of peace, be quartered in any house without the consent of the owner, nor in time of war except in the manner prescribed by law.

Treason. SEC. 16. Treason against the state shall consist only in levying war against it, adhering to its enemies, or giving them aid and comfort. No person shall be convicted of treason, unless on the evidence of two witnesses to the same overt act, or confession in open court.

Bail—punishments. SEC. 17. Excessive bail shall not be required; excessive fines shall not be imposed, and cruel and unusual punishment shall not be inflicted.

Eminent domain—drainage ditches and levees. SEC. 18. Private property shall not be taken for public use without just compensation first being made, or secured to be made to the owner thereof, as soon as the damages shall be assessed by a jury, who shall not take into consideration any advantages that may result to said owner on account of the improvement for which it is taken.

The general assembly, however, may pass laws permitting the owners of lands to construct drains, ditches, and levees for agricultural, sanitary or mining purposes across the lands of others, and provide for the organization of drainage districts, vest the proper authorities with power to construct and maintain levees, drains and ditches and to keep in repair all drains, ditches, and levees heretofore constructed under the laws of the state, by special assessments upon the property benefited thereby. The general assembly may provide by law for the condemnation of such real estate as shall be necessary for the construction and maintenance of such drains, ditches and levees, and prescribe the method of making such condemnation. Paragraph 2 added 1908, Amendment [13]

Imprisonment for debt. SEC. 19. No person shall be imprisoned for debt in any civil action, on mesne or final process, unless in case of fraud; and no person shall be imprisoned for a militia fine in time of peace.

Right of assemblage—petition. SEC. 20. The people have the right freely to assemble together to counsel for the common good; to make known their opinions to their representatives and to petition for a redress of grievances.

Attainder—ex post facto law—obligation of contract. SEC. 21. No bill of attainder, ex post facto law, or law impairing the obligation of contracts, shall ever be passed. Referred to in §12E.11, 16.2 of the Code

Resident aliens. SEC. 22. Foreigners who are, or may hereafter become residents of this state, shall enjoy the same rights in respect to the possession, enjoyment and descent of property, as native born citizens.

Slavery—penal servitude. SEC. 23. There shall be no slavery in this state; nor shall there be involuntary servitude, unless for the punishment of crime.

Agricultural leases. SEC. 24. No lease or grant of agricultural lands, reserving any rent, or service of any kind, shall be valid for a longer period than twenty years. Referred to in §461A.25 of the Code

Rights reserved. SEC. 25. This enumeration of rights shall not be construed to impair or deny others, retained by the people.

APPENDIX C
How Socialism Exploits Mankind

Socialism is a system of social organization that rejects the fact that goods are the fruits of the people's labor. The ownership of the means of producing goods provided by the people is claimed by secular authoritarians. They then use the power of government for laws to control the distribution of goods when, in fact, it is the freedom of the people to choose and buy goods made useful by others that gives direction for a healthy economy (supply and demand). Both the Webster and Random House dictionaries identify socialism as a "Marxist theory."

The following was written in 1916 by the Rev. William J. H. Boetcker, a Presbyterian clergyman and influential spokesman for American values:

You cannot bring about prosperity by discouraging thrift. You cannot strengthen the weak by weakening the strong.

You cannot help the poor man by destroying the rich.

You cannot further the brotherhood of man by inciting class hatred.

You cannot build character and courage by taking away man's initiative and independence.

You cannot help small men by tearing down big men.

You cannot lift the wage earner by pulling down the wage payer.

You cannot keep out of trouble by spending more than your income.

You cannot establish security on borrowed money.

You cannot help men permanently by doing for them what they will not do for themselves (www.quotationspage.com/quotes/William_J._H._Boetcker/.

Winston Churchill stated: "Socialism is inseparably interwoven with totalitarianism and the object worship of the state." He also said, "Socialism is a philosophy of failure, the creed of ignorance, and the gospel of envy, its inherent virtue is the equal sharing of misery" (Google, Winston Churchill quotes/w/winstonchurchill).

According to Alexis de Tocqueville in 1848: "Democracy [democratic republic] extends the sphere of individual freedom; socialism restricts it. Democracy [democratic republic] attaches all possible value to each man; socialism makes each man a mere agent, a mere number. [The two] have nothing in common but one word: equality. But notice the difference: while democracy seeks equality in liberty, socialism seeks equality in restraint and servitude" (Google, Alexis de Tocqueville Quotation/Quotations).

Appendix D
Citation Notes

Introduction

1. William Blackstone, *Commentaries on the Laws of England,* vol. I (Oxford: Clarendon Press,1765), 38–40.

2. Cited by Dinesh D'Souza, "Created Equal: How Christianity Shaped the West," Hillsdale College *Imprimis*, November 11, 2008.

3. George P. Shultz, Secretary of State under President Ronald Reagan, *Turmoil and Triumph.* This book traces the moral and economic collapse of the Soviet Socialist Empire. (New York: Macmillan, 1993), 1107.

4. Marvin Olasky, "God Doesn't Give Up," *World Magazine,* May 23, 2009, 64–67.

5. Benjamin Franklin, "Articles of Belief," in *The American Ideal of 1776,* ed. Hamilton Albert Long (Philadelphia: Heritage Books, 1963), 5.

Chapter 1

Citations left within the text

Chapter 2

6. Robert C. Winthrop, "A Model of Christian Charity," discourse

written aboard the *Arbella* during the voyage to Massachusetts, 1630, In *Life and Letters of John Winthrop*, 1867, 19.

7. Text version, Liberty Library, rendered into HTML by Jon Roland of the Constitution Society.

8. *The Rights of the Colonists* circulated by Adams in 1772, cited here by the Christian Defense Fund website (http://www.leaderu.com/orgs/cdf/onug/sadams.html).

9. Forrest McDonald, *Novus Ordo Seclorum: The Intellectual Origins of the Constitution* (Lawrence, KS: University of Kansas Press, 1985), 160.

10. *Articles of Confederation*, Article 1.

11. Pensacola Christian College, *United States History in Christian Perspective: Heritage of Freedom*, 2nd ed. (Pensacola, FL: A Beka Book, 1996), 112.

12. Harry Atwood, *The Constitution Explained*, 4th ed. (Merrimac, MA: Destiny Publishers, 1992,) 4.

13. http://www.americanrhetoric.com/speeches/benfranklin.htm.

14. Education Resources Information Center website, ED285786. Teaching about the *US Constitution* and the *Northwest Ordinance*.

15. The Northwest Ordinance www.earlyamerica.com/earlyamerica/milestones/ordinance/

16. David Barton, *Education and the Founding Fathers* (Aledo, Texas: WallBuilder Press, 1993), 4.

17. Catherine Drinker Bowen, *Miracle at Philadelphia: The Story of the Constitutional Convention* (Boston: Little, Brown, 1966), 139.

18. William L. Hickey, *The Constitution of the United States of America* (Philadelphia: Nabu Press, 1851), 188.

19. Library of Congress, "Primary Documents in American History," http://www.loc.gov/rr/program/bib/ourdocs/PrimDocsHome.html.

20. Atwood, The Constitution Explained, 5.

21. David Barton, *Original Intent: The Courts, the Constitution, and*

Religion (Aledo, TX: WallBuilder Press) 116. (Citing Washington, *Writings 1838,* Vol. X, 222–223, to John Armstrong on March 11, 1792).

22. Hamilton Albert Long, *The American Ideal of 1776*, (Philadelphia: Heritage Books, Inc., 1963), 205–206.

23. Gladstone speech, in *The North American Review*, (September, 1878), www.thefullwiki.org/William_Gladstone

Chapter 3

Citations left within the text

Chapter 4

24. *Zorach v. Clauson*, Docket 431, citation 343 US 306, 1952.

25. Donald S. Lutz, *The Origins of American Constitutionalism* (Baton Rouge, LA: Louisiana State University Press, 1988).

26. George Washington, Farewell Address, http://avalon.law.yale.edu/18th_ century/washing.asp.

27. James H. Hutson, *Religion and the Founding of the American Republic,* Washington, DC: Library of Congress, 1998, 84. The entire book is available at lastingsuccessedu.org).

28. Simon S. Montefiore, *Speeches That Changed the World,* (London: Quercus Publishing, 2005).

29. Benjamin Rush, Annals of Congress 1834, vol. I (September 25, 1789), 949–50.

30. Jared Sparks, ed., *The Writings of George Washington,* vol. 12 (Boston: Ferdinand Andrews, 1838), 119–20. (www.forbes.house.gov/uploadedfi les/Footnoted397.pdf).

31. Harry V. Jaffa, "In Defense of Political Philosophy," *National Review,* January 22, 1982, http://www.mmisi.org/ma/27_3-4/jaffa.pdf.

32. Barton, *Original Intent,* 118–19. See also *The Documentary History of the Supreme Court,* Vol. III, 436.

33. Ibid.

34. http://www.adherents.com/gov/Founding_Fathers_Religion.html/

Chapter 5

35. Alexander Hamilton, *Tully Papers*, 1794.

36. George Washington, *Farewell Address,* September 17, 1796, in *The Writings of George Washington* from the Original Manuscript Sources 1745–1799, published by the authority of Congress, ed. John C. Fitzpatrick, vol. 35, 214–38.

37. best-quotes-poems.com/George-Washington.html.

38. Thomas Jefferson, *Kentucky Resolutions,* 1798, in *The American Ideal of 1776,* ed. Hamilton Albert Long (Philadelphia: Heritage Books, 1963), 16–17.

39. Chief Justice John Roberts, discussing the role of Constitutional American politics with C-Span host Lamb on August 5, 2006.

40. Will and Ariel Durant, *The Story of Civilization,* the Solon of Athens "government by incalculable and changeable decrees Vol. II, *The Life of Greece,* 1939, 118.

41. William Ellery Channing, 1820, *The Great Doctrine of Retribution*: The Founders' Views of the Social Utility of Religion, cited by James H. Hutson in a presentation to the John Courtney Murray Seminar at the American Enterprise Institute, 1150 Seventeenth Street, N.W. Washington, DC June 6, 2000.

Chapter 6

42. http://en.wikiquote.org/wiki/Daniel_Webster

43. *Letters of John Quincy Adams to His Son*, www.americanchronicle.com/articles/view/48640.

44. Henry Steele Commager, forward to *McGuffey's Sixth Reader,* (New York: The American Library, 1962), xiv.

45. Daniel L. Dreisbach, Professor of Justice, Law, and Society at American University in Washington, DC, "How a Misused

Metaphor Changed Church–State Law, Policy, and Discourse," essay, Heritage Foundation publication, June 23, 2006, http://www. heritage.org/initiatives/first-principles.

46. Hutson, *Religion and the Founding of the American Republic,* 84.

47. V. P. Price "Are There Too Many Lawyers?" *Parade*, September 14, 2008, 9.

48. Thomas Jefferson, *Autobiography Notes on the State of Virginia, Addresses and Letters,* http://rationalspirituality.com/articles/Jaffa. htm)

49. John Dalberg, Letter to Bishop Mandell Creighton, an English historian refuting the dogma of papal infallibility, April 3, 1887.

50. http://www.layers-of-learning.com/2010/02/tenth-amendment-for-kids.html

51. Google search: Jeffrey Rosen, "Obstruction of Judges," *The New York Times*, August 11, 2002.

Chapter 7

52. John S. Brubacher and Willis Rudy, *Higher Education Transition* (New York: Harper and Row, 1958), 310.

53. Ibid., 296.

54. Ibid., 306.

55. W. T. Couch, *Academic Freedom,* (Washington, DC: Regnery Publishing, 1995), 1; quoted at a conference titled "Fifty Years After Russell Kirk's Academic Freedom: The Future of the Liberal Arts in America," Hillsdale College, Hillsdale, Michigan, February 2–6, 2005.

56. Kheel Center for Labor Management, *Teachers Union of the City of New York. Records,* 1921–42, Collection Number: 5445, Cornell University Library, Ithaca, NY, http://rmc.library.cornell.edu/EAD/htmldocs/KCL05445.html.

57. James Allen Johnson, "A Note on Academic Freedom: Schoolmen Must Declare Their Faith," *Phi Delta Kappan*, 44:185–88 (January,

1963), in Robert Hoffman, *Foundations of American Education,* (Boston: Allyn & Bacon, 1970), 192.

58. Will and Ariel Durant, *The Story of Civilization,* vol. 2, *The Life of Greece* (New York: Simon and Schuster,1939), 118.

59. Nathaniel F. Cabell, *Early History of the University of Virginia* as contained in the "Letters of Thomas Jefferson and Joseph B. Cabell," (n.p.: Richmond, Virginia, 1856), 339. Repeated in Hamilton Albert Long, *The American Ideal of 1778,* Your American Heritage Books, 141-44, 147.

60. Teresa Kay Albertson, "School District Cuts Not as Bad as Feared," *The Tribune* (Ames, IA), January 18, 2009, A3.

61. Peter Brimelow and Leslie Spencer, "How the National Education Association Corrupts Our Public Schools," *Forbes* magazine, June 7, 1993.

62. Dan Gearin, *"Schools Concerned with Union Bargaining Bill,"* The *Tribune* (Ames, IA), March 27, 2008, B4.

63. [a] J. Edgar Hoover, author of *Masters of Deceit,* served as director of the FBI for forty years. Published by the Kessinger Publishing, LLC in 1958. [b] D. L. Cuddy, PhD. author of *Chronology of Education with Quotable Quotes,* served as a senior assistant in the U. S. Department of Education (1982–88). Published by the Pro-Family Forum (5th edition, 1998), available *Radio Liberty,* Soquel, California. The book documents the strategy of leftists in public education by using statements from their own publications. The following example is a quote from a cosigner of the first *Humanist Manifesto,* published in 1933. He called for the "synthesizing of all religions" into "a socialized and cooperative economic order." [c] Fred C. Schwarz and David A. Noebel, authors of *You Can Still Trust the Communists ... to be Communists* (*socialists and Progressives too*). Published in 2010 by Christian Anti-Communism Crusade.

64. *Public Education Research and Analysis Communiqué* by the Education Intelligence Agency, Elk Grove, California, January 26, 2009.

65. Myron Lieberman, *Public Education: An Autopsy* (Cambridge: Harvard University Press), 1993.

Chapter 8

66. 66. Dr. J. Nelson Black, *Freefall of the American University* (Washington DC: WorldNetDaily, Books, 2004), xi.

67. See http://www.nhinet.org/bengtsson14-1.pdf for a review by Jan Olof Bengtson of Kimball's *Cultural Criticism.*

68. 68. Richard N. Ostling, *"Americans Important for Democrats,"* The Tribune (Ames, IA), August 28, 2004, B5.

Chapter 9

69. Milton and Rose Friedman, *Free To Choose* (New York: Harcourt Brace Jovanovich, 1980), 151.

70. State of Washington, *Kitsap Herald*, July 22, 2006, A4.

71. Dr. Soren Lovtrup, *Darwinism: The Refutation of a Myth* (New York: Croom Helm, 1987), 422.

72. Dr. Michael Ruse, *The Evolution-Creation Struggle* (Cambridge: Harvard University Press, 2005), 327.

73. atheism.about.com/.../michael-ruse-evolution-and-religion.htm

74. Adam Sedgwick (1785-1873) http://www.ucmp.berkeley.edu/history/sedgwick.html

75. Lawrence K. Altman, "One In Four US Teenage Girls Have STD's, Study Finds," *International Herald Tribune*, March 12, 2008 (www.myhealthnews.org/International_Herald_Tribune.../2008/.../12/

76. David Crary, *New York Associated Press*, February 28, 2008.

Chapter 10

77. John Eidsmore, *Christianity and the Constitution* (Grand Rapids, MI: Baker Publishing Group, 1987), 220.

78. Abigail Adams, Letter to John Quincy Adams, June 10, 1778, *Butterfield Adams Family Correspondence*, 3:37 (www.hist.cam.ac.uk/undergraduate/part2/2009.../special-subject-h.pdf).

79. Noah Webster, *American Dictionary of the English Language,* G.

and C. Merriam Company, 1828; cited by David A. Norris, *Lasting Success* (Ames, IA: Alpha Heartland Press, 2003), 7.

80. Cabell, Early History of the University of Virginia, 339.

Chapter 11

81. Abraham Lincoln, Speech at Edwardsville, Illinois, September 11, 1858, in Roy P. Basler, ed., *The Collective Works of Abraham Lincoln,* vol. 3 (Boston: 1935), 91–96. This speech is one of several Lincoln made against slavery *(http://rogerjnorton.com/Lincoln95. html, also http://quod.lib.umich.edu/l/lincoln/)*

Chapter 12

82. Ernest Renan's appeal to his agnostic friends, 1866, (http://www. questia.com/googleScholar.qst?docId=5002045047).

83. Peter Brimelow and Leslie Spencer, *How the National Education Association Corrupts Our Public Schools,* Forbes special publication, June 7, 1993.

84. Quotes from Marvin Olasky, "Academic Perestroika," World, December 5, 2009, www.worldmag.com/ marvinolasky?ndxpage=3.

85. Phyllis Schlafly, *The Supremacists: The Tyranny of Judges and How to Stop It* (Dallas: Spence Publishing Company, 2004), 14.

Index

Pages numbers in **bold** denote photos or pictures; with *n* denote note; with *illus* denote illustration.

A

AAUP (American Association of University Professors), 93, 94, 143, 144

Abel, 47

abortion, 25, 56, 72, 88, 101, 104, 107

academic freedom, 6, 86, 93, 94, 99, 117, 138, 140, 142, 143, 144

"Academic Freedom in the USA" (Standler), 144

Accuracy in Academia Campus Report (Beichman and Diggens), 103

ACLU (American Civil Liberties Union), 88, 143, 144

Adams, Abigail, 14, 91, **111**, 161

Adams, Jasper, 81

Adams, John, **14**, 17, 18, 40, 78, 91, 111, 121

Adams, John Quincy, 75, 91, 111

Adams, Samuel, 19, 36

adultery, 49, 72

AFL-CIO, 98, 122

Afrocentrism, 103

AFT (American Federation of Teachers), 94

agnosticism/agnostics, 120

alcoholism, 107

Alden, Rev. Mr. Timothy, 64

Allen, E., 132

Altman, Lawrence K., 108, 161

amendments, to Constitution, 5, 11, 18, 21, 24, 59, 60, 61, 70, 74, 86, 125, 126. *See also specific amendments*

American Association of University Professors (AAUP), 93, 94, 143, 144

American Civil Liberties Union (ACLU), 88, 143, 144

American conservatism, 5

American Federation of Teachers (AFT), 94

American ideal, 141

American philosophy of education, 95

American Pledge of Allegiance, 64

American principles
about, 101
One, 16
Two, 17
Three, 18
Four, 19
Five, 19

Six, 20
Seven, 22
Eight, 26
Nine, 27
Ten, 28
Eleven, 29
Twelve, 30
Thirteen, 31
Fourteen, 32
Fifteen, 33
American Prohibitory Act, 39
American Revolution, 128
American values (traditional)
   Boetcker as spokesman for, 153
   broadcasting of, 120
   compared to old European
     secular philosophy, 47
   courses on, 123
   defense of, 86
   gutting of, 6
   loss of, 56
   removing of, from classroom
     studies, 101
   turning students away from, 94
   war against, 89, 118
American Women's Association, 54
The American Crisis (Paine), 40
The American Ideal of 1776 (Long),
   57, 157
Ames Daily Tribune, vii, 132, 139,
   146
Ames IA, vii, 96, 132
anti-Americanism, 134, 139
anti-morality, 139
appeasement, 118
arbitrary rule, 63, 78
"Articles of Belief" (Franklin), 9,
   155
Articles of Confederation, 40, 41, 42,
   44, 58

atheism/atheists, 2, 3, 9, 47, 52, 54,
   62, 65, 79, 93, 104, 106, 139
atheistic belief, 47, 65
atheistic humanist approach, 138
atheistic revisionism, 3
atheistic sectarians, 16
atheistic-secular worldview, 4, 22,
   23, 33, 94, 95, 100, 101, 118,
   134, 142
*Autobiography Notes on the State of
   Virginia, Public and Private Papers,
   Address and Letters* (Jefferson), 83,
   159
Avalos, Hector, 139

B

Babel, 77
Bastiate, Frederic, 26
behavioral studies, 8, 137
Beichman, Arnold, 103
Bible
   benefits of, 47
   citations from. *See* scripture,
     citations from
   Governor Bradford and, 31
   importance of, to Founding
     Fathers, 59–60, 110
   knowledge of, 2
   as literature, 61
   and personal faith, 67
   on property ownership/wealth, 37
   quotes in Lincoln's second
     inaugural speech, 6
   study of, 35, 123
   truth from, 1
biblical principles, 64
Bill of Rights, 11, 18, 21, 24, 25, 48,
   64, 70, 74, 78, 85, 87
black studies, 103
Black's Law Dictionary, 71

Blackstone, William, 1, 22n, 59, 155
Bloom, Allan, 101
Boetcker, William J. H., 153
Bork, Robert, 89, 123
born again, 67
born-again Christians, 66
Boston Gazette, 17, 19
Boston Record, 132, 146
Bowling Green University, 99
Boy Scouts, attack on, 88
Braden, Kathleen, 55
Bradford, Governor, 31
Braintree Records, 32
Brandeis, Louis, 5
British government, 14
British Parliament, 39
Brubacher, John S., 23, 93, 159
Buckton, Margaret, 98
Burke, Edmund, 24, 48, 122
Burlamaqui, Jean-Jacques, 22*n*

C

Cain, 47
California Teachers Association, 89
Cambridge University, 107
campus mafia, 108
candidates for public office, 99, 122, 123, 125
capital punishment, 88
Capitol Building, 61, 82, 89
The Capitol, 64
Catholic hierarchy, 26
Catholics, 109
censorship, 86
Chambers, Whittaker, 4
Chandler, Robert, 117
Channing, William Ellery, 72, 158
charter schools, 122
China, 95
Christ

on cross of Calvary, 67
Webster's conversion to, 68
Christian private schools, 111
Christianity, 2, 4, 52, 54, 81, 106, 120, 126
Chronology of Education with Quotable Quotes (Cuddy), 98, 105, 160
church
colonial churches, 67
as third level of government, 37
Churchill, Winston, 154
church-state monopoly, 29, 30
citizen authority/control, 8, 28
citizen choice, 122
citizen involvement, 144
citizen paralysis, 117
citizens, responsibilities of, 38, 96
citizen-to-government disconnect, 75
civic religion, 66, 67
civic rights, 83
civil government
as fourth level of government, 37
as God instituted, 37
civil law, 49–50
civil religion, 58–65
civility, 22, 25
The Closing of the American Mind (Bloom), 101
Coercing Virtue: The Worldwide Rule of Judges (Bork), 123
collective bargaining, 97, 98, 99, 102, 109
colleges, 107, 142, 144
colonial churches, 67
The Coming Crisis in Citizenship: Higher Education's Failure to Teach America's History and Institutions, 56
Commager, Henry Steele, 80, 158

Commentaries on the Laws of England (Blackstone), 1, 59, 155

Commission on Excellence in Education, 55

Committee of Style and Arrangements, 43

communism/communists, 48, 75, 87, 88, 104

A Compilation of the Messages and Papers of the Presidents, 1789–1897 (Richardson), 53

compulsion, 139

Confederation of Congress, 40

Congressional Prayer Room, 65

conservatism/conservatives, 5, 6, 8, 80, 104, 118, 126, 136

Constitution of the State of Iowa, 17, 21, 135, 141

Constitution of the United States. See US Constitution

Constitutional Congress, 43

Constitutional Convention, 21, 29, 41, 42, 43, 76, 80, 126

constitutional revisionism, 62

contemporary liberalism, 101

Continental Army, 40

Continental Congress, ix, 14, 39, 40, 42, 60. *See also* First Continental Congress; Second Continental Congress

corruption, 69

creation science, 138

creationism/creationists, 66, 97

creation's God, 5, 30, 34, 53, 63, 69, 70, 78, 121, 124. *See also* God of creation

creation's nature, 1, 2, 3, 22*n*, 66, 77, 120. *See also* laws of creation's nature

crimes against society, 102

criminal law, 49–50

Cuba, 95

The Cube and the Cathedral (Weigel), 55

Cuddy, Dennis L., 98, 105, 160

cultural studies, 103

curriculum, 29, 66, 96, 111, 122

D

Darwin, Charles, 3, 5, 52, 54, 61, 79, 85, 93, 106, 107, 108

de Tocqueville, Alexis, 121, 154

death
  glorification of, 101
  and secular law, 23

Declaration of Independence, 5–6, 14–21, 24–33, 35, 40–41, 43–44, 58, 62–64, 70, 74, 80, 85, 95, 113, 121, 124

deconstruction, 103

Democrats, 55, 104, 131

Denver Post, 103, 132, 145

Des Moines Register, 132–133

Deuteronomy, 59

Dewey, John, 23, 52, 53, **54**, 93, 94, 100

Dickinson, John, 33

Dickinson College, ix

Diggens, John P., 103

Discourses Concerning Government (Sidney), 113

dishonesty, 4, 72

dissent, 6

A Dissertation on the Canon and Feudal Law (J. Adams), 17, 91, 121

diversity, 29, 56

divine origin, 16

domestic policy, 75

dorm cohabitation, 107, 137

Dostoevsky, Fyodor, 50

Douglas, Stephen A., 62

Douglas, William O., 58
Draft Kentucky Resolutions
(Jefferson), 27
Dred Scott v. Sanford, 81
drugs, 107, 131, 137
Durant, Ariel, 23, 71, 79, 158, 160
Durant, Will, 23, 71, 79, 158, 160

E

Earl Warren Court, 86, 87
economy, 25, 31, 48, 153
education
  American philosophy of, 95
  atheistic humanist approach to,
    138
  government education. *See*
    government education;
    government schools/
    government-run schools
  public education. *See* public
    education
  restoring educational traditions,
    120–121
  role of, 30
  secularized education, 50
  struggle within, 106
education guidelines, for University
  of Virginia, 96
Education Reporter, 55
education suppliers, competition of,
  29, 30
education tax, 7, 95, 127
educational freedom, 5
Einstein, Albert, 106, 111
Eisenhower, Dwight D., 64
election finance law, 27
An Election SERMON (Mayhew), 34
Eleventh Judicial District of Iowa
  grand jury, 131–134, 136, 140
Elliot, John, 16

Elliot's Debates, The Debates In The
  Several State Conventions Adoption
  Of The Federal Constitution (Elliot),
  16
Emancipation Proclamation, 40
emotions, 4, 101, 112, 113
Encyclopedia Britannica, 106, 110
Engels, Frederick, 53
"Essay Concerning Human
  Understanding" (Locke), 59
Essay Concerning the True Original
  Extent and End of Civil Government
  (Locke), 113
Essay: Who Are the Keepers of the
  People's Liberties? (Madison), **11**
euthanasia, 101
Everson v. Board of Education, 6, 8,
  53, 55, 82, 83, 86, 107, 126
evil
  absorbing details of, 96
  differences between good and
    evil, 23, 101
  laws of good and evil, 1–2
  open-mindedness as, 23
  protection from, 25
  punishments for, 49
  revisionist morality as, 5
  storming strongholds of, 85
  triumph of, 122
  union monopolies and, 8
  victory over, 2, 119
  ways of men, 26
evil life practices, 29, 56
evolution/evolutionists, 97, 105,
  106, 139
The Evolution-Creation Struggle
  (Ruse), 106, 161
exploitation, 23

F

family
attacks on the, 53, 88, 144
breakdown of, 107
enemies of, 17, 29, 50, 96
obligations of, 72
preservation of, 110
as second level of government,
36–37
traditional family, 18, 97, 113,
117, 122, 127
wholeness of, 16
Farewell Address (Washington), 22,
27, 28, 60, 69, 74, 113, 157, 158
The Farmer Refuted (Hamilton), 18
fascism/fascists, 8, 25, 63, 75, 79,
98, 99
Federal Republic, 70
federalism, 32, 75
The Federalist Papers, 11, 17, 28, 31,
32, 60, 67, 70, 80, 84, 113
feel-good emotions, 101
feminist agenda, 88, 103
Field v. School District, 51
Fifth Amendment, 59
First Amendment, 42, 62, 69, 82,
83, 89, 97, 98, 121, 126
First Congregational Church of
Washington, 61
First Continental Congress, 13, 30,
39, 111
First Principle, 2–9, 16, 110, 121
foreign nations, 88
Founding Fathers, 1, 13, 21, 22, 33,
41, 47, 58, 59, 64, 66, 67, 72, 76,
78, 80, 110, 111, 120
Founding Mothers, 91
Fourteenth Amendment, 59, 61
France, government charters of, 46
Franklin, Benjamin, **9**, 42, 76, 77,
79, 155

free enterprise system, 97
free speech, 69
Free to Choose (M. and R.
Friedman), 105, 161
freedom
academic freedom. *See* academic
freedom
of choice, 3
compared to slavery, 26, 39
costs of, 119
as cultural value, 85
democracy and, 154
denial of, 65
and the economy, 153
educational freedom, 5
guarantor of, 16
liberty and, 20
for religious competition, 53
religious freedom, 5, 43, 62, 66,
82
right to choose, 36
source of, 2
of speech, 29
Freedom in Iowa (Iowa Civil
Liberties Union), 133, 136, 143
Freedom Ordinance, 42
French Revolution, 48, 120
Friedman, Milton, 105, 161
Friedman, Rose, 105, 161
Fundamental Orders of
Connecticut, 36

G

Gates, Bill, 111
gay studies, 103
Gen. 49, 60
gender-specific organizations, attack
on, 88
Genovese, Eugene, 103
George Washington's Sacred Fire
(Lillback), 60

The Gettysburg Address, 21, 65
Geyer, Georgie Anne, 103
G.I. Bill, 7
Gingrich, Newt, 6
Gladstone, William E., 46, 59, 157
glasnost, 3
God
  accountability to, 38
  belief in, 13, 117
  denial of belief in, 66
  elimination of references to, 53,
    77, 79, 101, 108
  laws of, 3n
  and marriage, 37
  public acclaim of, 88
  as source of unalienable rights, 17
  sovereignty of, 38
  and teaching of American history,
    6
  war against, 6, 52, 76, 89
  Washington on, 60
  will of, 4, 114
God of creation, 1, 2, 6, 33, 45, 48,
  61, 64, 80, 83, 108, 110. *See also*
  creation's God
"God save America," 124
God-given rights, 20, 25, 48, 72,
  80, 102
God-honoring
  character-building booklets, 95
  Declaration of Independence, 44,
    50, 119
  faith, 89
  goals, 113
  law, 45
  meaning for government of laws,
    and not of men, 79
  natural-law philosophy, 22
  predicate of the Constitution, 3,
    5
  principles, 21, 119

  private schools, 122
  religious nature, 16
God-ordained authorities, 36, 37
God-rejecting
  atheism as, 65
  intellectuals, 4
  theory of evolution, 139
  worldview, 5n, 54, 94, 101, 118,
    121
God's Word, 35, 49
God-to-man cooperative, 67
Golden Rule, 1
A Golden Treasury from the Bible
  (NEA), 95*illus*
Gonzalez, Guillermo, 139
good, differences between good and
  evil, 23, 101
Gorbachev, Mikhail, 3
Gorbachev, Raisa, 3n
government
  big government, 19, 36, 69
  debt of, 32
  decentralization of, 28
  by incalculable and changeable
    decree, 23, 48, 51, 71, 72, 79,
    82, 95, 101
  limited government, 28
  limited governments, 31, 37, 50,
    63, 70, 73, 76, 102, 120
  powers of, 20–21, 31, 43, 73–74,
    75
  purpose of, 45
  servants of, as accountable to
    God, 38
  teaching of, 113
  as a tool, 63
  by written and permanent law,
    72, 101, 109
government education. *See also*
  government schools/government-
  run schools

contrasted with public education, 6

functions of, 66

promise of reforms made by, 109

government of laws

described, 77

Hamilton on, 69

and not of men, 22, 78, 79, 81, 83, 125

government schools/government-run schools, 29, 30, 51, 88, 126. *See also* government education

grace, 67, 114

Graham, Catherine Macaulay, 45

Grand Jury Presentment *Problems in Higher Education*, 134–142, 145

Grant, George, 53

Great Reformation, 2

Great Seal of the United States, 65

Grotius, Hugo, 22*n*

H

Halley, Henry H., 59

Halley's Bible Handbook (Halley), 59

Hamilton, Alexander, 17, 18, 23, 31, **39**, 52, 60, 67, 69, 84, 158

happiness, pursuit of, 1, 3, 13, 15, 17, 18, 29, 30, 32, 33, 42, 48, 60, 62, 71, 78, 81, 85

hard sciences, 87, 96, 97

hard work, 35

Harvard University, 68

Hayek, Friedrich A., 138

Heartland Foundation, Inc., 122

Higher Authority, 17, 70, 78, 79, 80, 83, 85, 124

Higher Education Transition (Brubacher and Rudy), 23, 159

history, teaching of, 6, 56, 67, 86, 97, 113, 117

Hitler, Adolf, 61

homeschooling, 111, 122

homosexuality, 27, 55, 56, 104, 107

honesty, 137

Hoover, Herbert, 115

Hoover, J. Edgar, 98, 160

Horowitz, David, 117

hospitals, abundance of, 36, 107

human authoritarianism, 64

Humanist Manifesto, 52, 94, 160

The Humanist, 54

humility, 1, 128

Hutson, James H., 47, 61, 157, 159

Huxley, Thomas, 59

I

ideological competition, 79, 86

illicit sex, 137

illiteracy, 105

immorality, 131

"In God We Trust," 6, 13, 47, 66, 75, 101

Independence Hall, 15

individual rights, 102

The Intellectual Origins of the Constitution (McDonald), 26

intelligent design, 108, 139

intelligible design, 110

Iowa, Eleventh Judicial District grand jury, 131–134, 136, 140

Iowa Association of School Boards, 98

Iowa Board of Regents, 132, 140–141

Iowa Civil Liberties Union, 133, 136

Iowa Family Policy Center News Letter, 55

Iowa legislature, 98

Iowa State University, 131, 136, 138, 139

Iowa State University Press, 133, 136, 143
Iowa Supreme Court, 133
Israelites, 38
ISU Atheist Society, 139
Italy, government charters of, 46

J
Jaffa, Harry V., 63
Jay, John, 84, **111**
Jefferson, Thomas, 20, 25, 27, 28, 30, **61**, 71, 82, 83, 96, 113, 158, 159
Jefferson Memorial, 82
Jenner, William E., 87
John Adams (McCullough), 14
Journal (Noebel), 117
Judeo-Christian principles, 1, 101
judges
   appointment of, 123
   authoritarian judges, 147
   chronology of actions of, 88
   conservative judges, 126
   duty of, 83
   indoctrination of law students who become, 104
   liberal judges, 23, 80, 88, 124, 126
   liberal judges-turned legislators, 56
   radical judges, 144
   roles of, 17, 24, 25, 63, 75, 80–81, 83, 84–85, 123, 126
   ruled by incalculable and changeable decrees, 82
   self-indulgent judges, 69
   supremacist judges, 49, 56, 76, 125
   truly fine judges, 73
   unelected judges, 81, 82, 83, 123, 125

judicial incompetence, 77
judicial independence, 25, 125
judiciary
   as branch of government, 84
   defilement of, 73–89
   pervasiveness of federal judiciary, 21, 25
justice, ix, 20, 21, 39, 45, 67, 75. *See also* social justice

K
Kampf, Louis, 103
Kandell, I. L., 134
Kansas House of Representatives, 117
The Keyes of This Blood (Martin), 103
Keynes, John Maynard, 52
Kimball, Roger, 103
King George III, 121
King John, 69
King of England, 35, 38, 39
King of Kings, 32, 120
Kurtz, Paul, 52

L
labor, 31, 32, 37, 48, 153
labor unions, 98, 122. *See also* teachers unions
Lacanian analysis, 103
law
   civil law, 49–50
   criminal law, 49–50
   man-made law, 23
   moral law, 76, 78, 97, 110
   moral predicate for, 52, 62, 69, 70, 73, 77–80, 81, 119
   natural law, 23
   Revealed Law, 59
   Rule of Law/rule of law, 50, 51, 63, 78, 85, 101, 123, 126
   secular law, 23

study of, 29
teacher tenure law. *See* teacher
tenure law
The Law (Bastiat), 26
law enforcement, 88, 139–140. *See
also* police
law professors, 23, 77, 126, 147
laws of creation's nature, 2, 3, 36,
37, 49, 75, 97
laws of man, 3, 23, 49
Laws of Nature and of Nature's
God, 1, 22, 59
lawyers
conservative lawyers, 126
leftist lawyers, 85
laziness, 37
Lectures (Wilson), 20, 25, 33
Left Eclecticism, 103
leftist takeover, 95
leftists, 7, 8, 29, 51, 55, 75, 85, 88,
94, 97, 98, 100, 102, 104, 118,
120, 136, 139, 143, 144, 147
Legacy of Planned Parenthood
(Grant), 53
legal studies, 103
liberals, 3, 23, 48, 52n, 56, 62, 74,
76, 77, 79, 80, 81, 83, 88, 99,
101, 103, 104, 118, 124, 126, 133
liberation theology, 103
liberty, 1, 3, 5, 8, 13, 14, 15, 16, 17,
18, 19, 20, 21, 24, 25, 26, 28, 29,
30, 31, 36, 40, 42, 45, 48, 51, 59,
62, 66, 69, 70, 71, 72, 75, 76, 82,
83, 85, 86, 91, 94, 95, 102, 110,
118, 120, 121, 124, 134, 144,
147, 154. *See also* religious liberty
Liberty Bell, 15
Lieberman, Myron, 99, 160
life, principle of, 24, 25, 29, 32
Lillback, Peter A., 60

limited civil governments, 28, 31,
37, 50, 63, 70, 73, 76, 102, 120
Lincoln, Abraham, 1, 21, 40, 59,
62, **63**, 80, 82, 110, 118, 162
Lincoln Memorial Statue, 7
Lincoln-Douglas debates, 62
Lippman, Walter, 105
"living constitution," 50
local control, 75, 96
Locke, John, 59, 113
London, Herbert, 103
Long, Hamilton Albert, 15, 56–57,
157
Loning Historical Reference Works,
22n
Los Angeles Times, 89
Lovtrup, Soren, 106, 161
Lusk Laws, 94
Lutz, Donald S., 58

M

MacArthur, Douglas, 119
Madison, James, **11**, 15, 18, 26, 28,
41, 60, 67, 70, 84, 96, 113
Magna Carta, 69
*Manifesto of the Communist Party,
1848* (Mark and Engels), 53
man-made law, 23
Marbury v. Madison, 22, 78, 80, 84,
85, 86
marriage
obligations of, 72
same-sex, 25, 104
Sanger on, 53
traditional, 19, 37, 49, 89, 101,
134
war against, 88
Marshall, John, 22, 78, 81, 84
Marshall Plan, 119
Martin, Malachi, 103
Marx, Karl, 3, 31, 52, 53, 112

Marxism/Marxists, 102, 103, 104, 117

Massachusetts Constitution, 78–79

Masters of Deceit (J. Hoover), 98, 160

Mayflower Compact, 35

Mayhew, Jonathan, 34

McCullough, David, 14

McDonald, Forrest, 26

Meany, George, 98, 122

media, 56, 132, 136

Medieval Europe, 6, 30, 109

Modern Languages Association, 103

Montesquieu, 59

moral absolutes, 23, 50, 51, 81, 97, 126

moral judgment, 50, 62

moral law, 76, 78, 97, 110

moral pollution, 30, 132, 141

moral predicate for law, 52, 62, 69, 70, 73, 77–80, 81, 119

moral relativism, 3, 50, 104

moral responsibilities, 38

moral revisionism, 53

morality, 8, 22, 30, 42, 48, 50, 54, 60, 61, 64, 65, 75, 78, 80, 89, 106, 117, 118, 127, 134, 139, 140. *See also* revisionist morality

Morris, Governor, 43

Moses, 72, 78

N

A Nation at Risk (Commission on Excellence in Education), 55

National Civic Literacy Board, University of Connecticut, 56

National Day of Prayer, 13, 62, 124

National Education Association (NEA), 8, 55, 89, 94, 95, 97, 98–99

National Health and Nutrition Examination Survey, 108

National Labor Relations Act (NLRB), 143

natural law, 23

Natural Rights of Marriage (Wilson), 19

natural-law philosophy, 22, 23

Nature's God, 22n

The Nature of the American System (Rushdoony), 33

NEA (National Education Association), 8, 55, 89, 94, 95, 97, 98–99

neo-Marxism, 103

Nevada Journal, 132, 145

New Hampshire, 44

new historicism, 103

"New Left's Boasts: We Are Organizing Sedition," 138

New Testament, 59

New York Times, 138

Newcombe, Jerry, 60

Newton, Sir Isaac, 59

Nietzsche, Friedrich, 52

1940 Statement of Principles on Academic Freedom and Tenure (AAUP), 143

Nitezsche, Friedrich, 2

NLRB (National Labor Relations Act), 143

NLRB v. Yeshiva University, 143

Noebel, David A., 98, 102, 160

Northwest Ordinance, 42, 89, 95, 156

O

Olasky, Marvin, 4, 155

old European secular philosophy, 4, 5, 47, 52n, 54–55, 82, 93, 95, 99, 101, 103, 107, 118, 124

Old Testament, 59, 72
Olive Branch Petition, 39
"On Civil Government" (Locke), 59
On the Origin of Species (Darwin),
  5n, 54, 61, 106, 107, 108
one nation under God, 124
open-mindedness, 23, 82, 85, 94,
  95
oppression, 19, 28, 33, 78, 147
*The Organic Laws of the United States
  of America*, 123
Organization of American
  Historians, 103

P

Paine, Thomas, 40
parents
  authority of, 97, 105, 110, 140,
    144
  education tax routed through, 7,
    122, 144
  responsibilities of, 37, 110, 140
  rights of, 30, 51, 142
  roles of, 36
Parks, Robert, 133
Paterson, Judge, 64
patriotism/patriots, ix, 6, 33, 60,
  101, 122
Pennsylvania Herald, 43
Pennsylvania Ratifying Convention,
  15
perestroika, 3n
personal faith, 58, 66–68
personal responsibility, 20, 35, 69
Pew Center on the States, 109
Pilgrims, 35
Pinckney, Charles, **46**
Planned Parenthood, 53
Pledge of Allegiance, 88, 124, 126
Plymouth Colony, 31

police, 36, 139. *See also* law
  enforcement
political activism, 1
political adventurism, 23
political circumvention, 144
political correctness, 29, 48, 134
political science, 4n, 6, 97, 117
Poole, Ben, 123
popular culture, 89
pornography, 88
poststructuralism, 103
Potter, C. F., 100
poverty, 4, 37, 72
prayer, practice of, 42, 76–77, 79,
  104, 126, 128
principles
  American principle One, 16
  American principle Two, 17
  American principle Three, 18
  American principle Four, 19
  American principle Five, 19
  American principle Six, 20
  American principle Seven, 22
  American principle Eight, 26
  American principle Nine, 27
  American principle Ten, 28
  American principle Eleven, 29
  American principle Twelve, 30
  American principle Thirteen, 31
  American principle Fourteen, 32
  American principle Fifteen, 33
  American principles, overall, 101
  biblical principles, 64
  First Principle, 16, 110, 121
  God-honoring, 21, 119
  Judeo-Christian principles, 1, 101
  of life, 24, 25, 29, 32
  responsibility-authority-control
    principle, 140
  of scripture, 78
prisons

abundance of, 36, 107
America's rank as incarcerator,
109
privacy rights, 56
private schools, 111, 122
property ownership, 30, 31, 37
Proposition 8 (California), 89
prosperity, 16, 17, 22, 23, 45, 60,
85, 120, 153
Protestant hierarchy, 26
Public Education: An Autopsy
(Lieberman), 99
public education. *See also*
education; government education;
government schools/government-
run schools
Brandeis on, 5–6
and civic religion, 66, 83
contrasted with government
education, 6
control of, 89
cost of, 144
courts as enemy of traditional
culture in, 89
described, 94
Dewey as father of, 53
direction of, 142
failures of, 75
gutting of traditional American
values in, 6
lexicon of, 1
Marxism and, 102
quality of, 144
radicals in the soft sciences in,
131
study of problems in, 55
Public Education: An Autopsy
(Lieberman), 160

Q

Quotes by John Dickinson
(Dickinson), 33

R

Radical Son (Horowitz), 117
radicals, 4, 6, 8, 27, 29, 30, 51, 52,
53, 71, 82, 86, 88, 89, 98, 103,
104, 105, 108, 109, 117, 131,
132, 136–138, 140, 141, 143, 144
Randolph, Edmund Jennings, 41,
43, 77
Rationalism, 120
Reagan, Ronald, 36
reality, illusion of, 51*illus*
rebellion, 36, 85, 139
*Reflections on the Revolution in
France* (Burke), 48
Reformation, 2, 109, 123
*Religion and the Founding of the
American Republic* (Hutson), 47,
61, 157, 159
religious freedom, 5, 43, 62, 66, 82
religious liberty, 30, 69, 83
Reminiscences and Reflections (R.
Gorbachev), 3n
Renan, Ernest, 120
Republicans, 89, 104, 131
republics, 28, 40, 42, 43, 70, 84,
95, 154
Response Magazine, 55
responsibility-authority-control
principle, 140
Revealed Law, 59
revisionist history, 101
revisionist morality, 3, 5, 79, 101,
127
Revolutionary Army, 41
Richardson, David B., 103
Richardson, James D., 52
right to choose, 16

The Road to Serfdom (Hayek), 138
Roberts, John, 71, 84, 158
Roe v. Wade, 88
Roman Catholic Church, 109
Roosevelt, Franklin D., 98, 122
Rudy, Willis, 23, 93, 159
Rule of Law/rule of law, 50, 51, 63,
  78, 85, 101, 123, 126
rule of man, 45, 51, 63, 82, 101
Ruse, Michael, 106, 161
Rush, Benjamin, ix, 61, 157
Rushdoony, R. J., 33

S

same-sex marriage, 25, 104
Sanger, Margaret, 53, **54**
SAT (Scholastic Aptitude Test), 56
Satan, 36, 37, 48
Scalia, Antonin, 83
Schlafly, Phyllis, 86, 87, 162
Scholastic Aptitude Test (SAT), 56
school boards, 8, 51, 96, 97, 98,
  123
schools. *See also* colleges; education;
  universities
    charter schools, 122
    homeschooling, 111, 122
    private schools, 111, 122
Schwarz, Fred C., 98, 160
science, 29, 79, 106, 107, 110. *See
also* creation science; hard sciences;
  political science; soft sciences
scripture, citations from
  Acts 5:29, 5
  2 Chron. 7:14, 128
  2 Cor. 1, 23
  2 Cor. 3:17, 1
  2 Cor. 5:17, 66
  Dan. 4:37, 38
  Deut. 5, 49
  Eccl. 12:1, 95

Esp. 5:22–33, 37
Esp. 6:1, 4, 37
Exod. 20, 49
Exod. 20:1–17, 61
Gen. 2:23-24, 18
Gen. 3:13, 96
Isa. 5:15–16, 96
Isa. 5:20, 96
Isa. 10:28–31, 67
Isa. 33:22, 59
James 1:12–17, 96
Jer. 17, 59
John 3:16–17, 67
1 John 3:17, 37
Matt. 5–7, 61
Matt. 18:16–19, 37
1 Pet. 1:23, 66
1 Pet. 2:13–14, 37
Prov. 3:5–6, 6
Prov. 10:4–5, 37
Prov. 15:5, 37
Prov. 29:2, 64
Prov. 30, 95
Prov. 31:13–27, 37
Ps. 75:7, 38
Ps. 119:105, 65
Rom. 5:8–9, 67
Rom. 10:9–13, 67
Rom. 13:1–3, 36
Rom. 13:1–4, 37, 38
Rom. 13:3–4, 37
Rom. 13:6, 38
Rom. 16:19, 96
1 Sam. 8, 38
2 Thess. 3:10–11, 31
1 Tim. 5:8, 37
1 Tim. 5:17, 37
scripture, principles of, 78
Second Continental Congress, 9,
  14, 39, 40
secret ballot, 24

secular, use of word, 4–5
secular academician, 48
secular adventurism, 81
secular agenda, 24
secular authoritarians, 29, 50
secular educators, 3
secular elitists, 72
secular humanism, 5, 54, 100
Secular Humanist Manifesto (Potter), 100
secular law, 23
secular militants, 5, 6, 65, 66, 76, 79, 86, 117, 118, 121, 126
secular progressives, 7, 8
secularized education, 50
Sedgwick, Adam, 107, 161
self-defense, 40
self-government, 8, 23, 24, 29, 36, 55, 63, 80, 82, 86, 96, 110
self-reliance, 16, 20, 21, 37, 45, 102, 127
self-rule, 17, 48, 75, 94, 126
Senate Subcommittee on Internal Security, 87
separation of powers, 23–24, 43, 59, 70, 81, 83, 84
Sermon on the Mount, 61
sexual information, 51
sexual modesty, 53
sexual virtue, 101, 137
sexuality, 89
sexually transmitted diseases (STDs), 108
Shadow World (Chandler), 117
Sidney, Algernon, 113
sin, 4, 67, 101
sinful nature, of man, 26, 44
slavery, 11, 23, 26, 33, 39, 40, 42
"So help me God," 60
social action materialism, 103
social engineering, 102

social justice, 29, 56
socialism/socialists, 74, 117, 153–154
sodomy, 25
soft sciences, 4n, 7, 29, 65, 75, 86, 87, 96, 97, 137, 144
Solon of Athens, 23, 71, 72, 79, 95
sovereignty of man under God over government, 3, 13, 16, 19, 124
Soviet Union, 3, 95
Speeches That Changed the World (Montefiore), 61, 157
The Spirit of Laws (Montesquieu), 59
spiritual glory, 85
Spurgeon, Charles, 26
Stacey, Judith, 53
Stalin, Joseph, 61
Stamp Act, 17
Standler, Ronald B., 144
stare decisis, 89, 126
"The Star-Spangled Banner," 46, 115
State of Iowa Bill of Rights, 147–151
state-church monopoly, 29, 30
STDs (sexually transmitted diseases), 108
stealing, 23, 52n, 72
The Story of Civilization, Vol. II, The Life of Greece (W. and A. Durant), 23, 79, 158, 160
strategic priorities, 120–128
structuralism, 103
suicide, 89, 101, 126
superintendents, 86, 96, 98
The Supremacists: The Tyranny of Judges and How to Stop It (Schlafly), 86, 87, 88, 162
Supreme Court. *See* US Supreme Court

Supreme Court Interim Opinion, 125, 126
survey scores, 56

T

tax revenues, 21
taxation without representation, 39
taxes, 31–32, 52*n*, 88, 95, 102, 122, 127
taxpayer expense, 53, 136, 137
taxpayer objections, 100
taxpayer revenues, 7, 58, 66, 70, 74, 79, 88, 94, 104, 113, 118, 122, 127
taxpayer support, 50
taxpayers. *See also* taxpayer expense; taxpayer objections; taxpayer revenues; taxpayer support
  authority of, 71, 144
  responsibilities of, 140
  rights of, 138, 142
Tea Party, 39
teacher contracts, 8, 97, 98, 118, 143, 144
teacher tenure guarantees, 4, 8, 9, 25, 53, 93, 97, 118, 141, 142
teacher tenure law, 6, 29, 30, 75, 85–86, 93, 96, 102, 104, 107, 109, 122, 144
teachers
  bad teachers, 8, 98
  good teachers, 76, 86, 87, 122
  leftist teachers, 51, 144
  pro-family, pro-life, pro-American, 87
  radical teachers, 29, 30, 52, 53, 88, 89, 104, 109, 117, 143, 144
  rights of, 118
  tenure. *See* teacher tenure law
  unions. *See* teachers unions

Teachers Association of California, 89
teachers unions, 6, 7, 8, 30, 86, 88, 96, 107, 118, 122, 142
The Teachers' Unions: How the NEA and AFT Sabotage Reform and Hold Students, Parents, Teachers, and Taxpayers Hostage to Bureaucracy (Lieberman), 99
Ten Commandments, 1, 48, **49**, 50, 61, 72, 83, 88, 89, 104
Tenth Amendment, 32, 86, 104
test scores
  decline of, 93
  Scholastic Aptitude Test (SAT), 56
theistic belief, 47, 65
Torcaso v. Watkins, 5
totalitarian governments, 69
traditional American values. *See* American values (traditional)
traditional culture, 89
traditional family, 18, 97, 113, 117, 122, 127
traditional values, 101
The Tribune, 86
Truman, Harry, 104
truth, 2, 16, 30, 34, 37, 47, 48, 54, 56, 64, 75, 85, 93–94, 97, 101, 139, 142
Tully Papers (Hamilton), 23, 69, 158
tyranny, 2, 4, 28, 36, 41, 45, 75, 78, 82, 102, 119, 123, 142
tyranny of the mind, 98
tyrants of the mind, 30

U

The Ugly Liberal American (Wheeler), 57, 119
Uhlenhopp, Harvey, 133

unalienable rights, 17, 19, 25, 30,
43, 45, 48, 63, 71, 80, 83
"under God," 64
Understanding the Times (Noebel),
102
union monopolies, 7, 8, 29, 54, 63,
102, 109
United Nations, 3
universities, 107, 132, 142, 144
University of California at Davis, 53
University of Connecticut, 56
University of Pennsylvania, ix
University of Virginia, 96, 113
US, Great Seal of, 65
US Capitol, 64
US Census Bureau, 105
US Congress, 18, 27, 64, 65, 123,
124, 126
US Constitution
adherence to, 17
amendments, 5, 18, 60, 74
compared to charters of other
nations, 70
and the *Declaration of
Independence*, 62
Everson v. Board of Education, 8
Fifth Amendment, 59
First Amendment, 42, 62, 69, 82,
83, 89, 97, 98, 121, 126
Fourteenth Amendment, 59, 61
Franklin as signer of, 9
Gladstone on, 46
God-honoring predicate of, 3
and government of men, 79
intent of, 50
interpreting the meaning of, 25
and Lusk Laws, 94
Madison as principal author of,
11
as one of America's most
important charters, 58

as political document, 101
and the political truth, 72
Preamble to, 20, 21, 45
proposed, 44
quotation from, 29
as replacement for *Articles of
Confederation*, 42
resolutions for, 43
retaining original meaning of, 83
as rule of law document, 123
and separation of powers, 24
signing of, **44**
Ten Commandments, 104
Tenth Amendment, 32, 86
underpinning of, 23
Wilson as signer of, 15
US Court of Appeals, 51
US National Academy of Science,
105
US News and World Report, 103
US Supreme Court
described, 125
Dred Scott v. Sanford, 81
Earl Warren Court, 87
Everson v. Board of Education, 6,
53, 55, 82, 83, 86, 107, 126
justices, 73
liberal majorities on, 3
Marbury v. Madison, 78, 80–81,
84, 85, 86
NLRB v. Yeshiva University, 143
as not the supreme authority,
76–77
review of eighty-seven precedents,
64
Roe v. Wade, 88
sculpture of Moses and Ten
Commandments, 49, 72
secular majorities on, 7
Torcaso v. Watkins, 5
USA Today/Gallup Poll, 13

utopia, 112, 120

V

Valley Forge, 40, 81
Vanderbur, Charles, 131
Vietnam, 104
Virginia Declaration of Rights, 30
Virginia Resolutions of 1799, 113
Virginia Statute of Religious Liberty,
  56
virtue, 1, 22, 34, 35, 62, 63, 72,
  111, 117, 120, 137, 154
voting, 20, 24, 29, 45, 52*n*, 77, 83,
  104, 144

W

"wall of separation" metaphor, 82
Wall Street Journal, 98
War for Independence, 41, 81
Washington, George, 22, 27, 28,
  40, 41, 42, 44, 45, 60, 62, 69, 71,
  74, 113, 157, 158
The Washington Times, 53
"We the People," 21, 43, 45
wealth, 29, 37, 52*n*
Weaver, Reg, 89
Webster, Daniel, 75
Webster, Noah, **67**, 112, 161
Webster's Blue-Back Speller, 112
Webster's Dictionary, 50, 112, 113
Weigel, George, 55
well-educated students, described,
  113–114
Wheatley, John, 40
Wheatley, Phillis, 40
Wheatley, Susanna, 40
Wheeler, Jack, 57, 119
Whitefield, George, 40
Williams, William A., 103
Wilson, James, **15**, 19, 20, 25, 33
Winthrop, John, 35, 36

Witness (Chambers), 4
The Woman Rebel, 53
Women's studies, 103, 117
work ethic, 21, 22, 30, 31, 45
The Works of Edmund Burke (Burke),
  122

Y

*You Can Still Trust the Communists
  … to Be Communists (Socialists
  and Progressive Too)* (Schwarz and
  Noebel), 98, 160
youth, as victims, 104, 109

Z

Zogby International, 56